BOOKS BY ANN SPANGLER

Daily Secrets of the Christian Life, Hannah Whitall Smith (compiled by Ann Spangler)
Don't Stop Laughing Now! compiled by Ann Spangler and Shari MacDonald
He's Been Faithful, Carol Cymbala with Ann Spangler
Look Who's Laughing! compiled by Ann Spangler and Shari MacDonald
Men of the Bible, coauthored with Robert Wolgemuth
She Who Laughs, Lasts! compiled by Ann Spangler
Women of the Bible, coauthored with Jean Syswerda
Women of the Bible: 52 Stories for Prayer and Reflection

BOOKS BY SHARI MACDONALD

A Match Made in Heaven
Don't Stop Laughing Now! compiled by Ann Spangler and Shari MacDonald
Humor for a Woman's Heart, compiled by Shari MacDonald
Humor for the Heart, compiled by Shari MacDonald
Look Who's Laughing! compiled by Ann Spangler and Shari MacDonald
Love on the Run
The Perfect Wife

Rib-Tickling Stories of Fun, Faith, Family, and Friendship

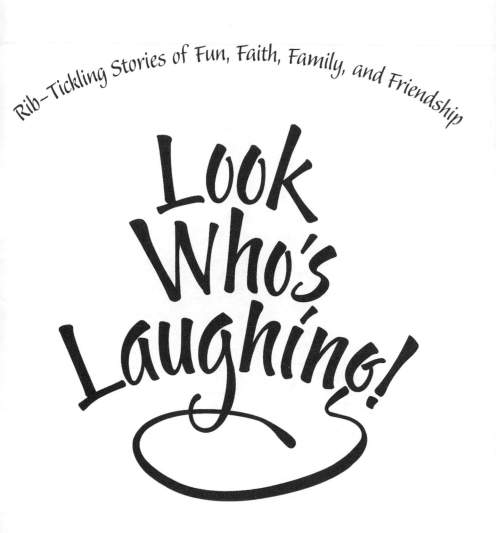

Look Who's Laughing!

Compiled by Ann Spangler & Shari MacDonald

Stories by: Barbara Johnson Patsy Clairmont John Ortberg
Chonda Pierce Becky Freeman Marilyn Meberg Luci Swindoll

ZONDERVAN™

GRAND RAPIDS, MICHIGAN 49530 USA

ZONDERVAN™

Look Who's Laughing!
Copyright © 2003 by Ann Spangler

Requests for information should be addressed to:
Zondervan, *Grand Rapids, Michigan 49530*

Library of Congress Cataloging-in-Publication Data

Look who's laughing! : rib-tickling stories of fun, faith, family, and friendship /
compiled by Ann Spangler and Shari MacDonald.
    p. cm.
  ISBN 0-310-24692-X
  1. Religion — Humor.   2. Conduct of life — Humor.   I. Spangler, Ann.
II. MacDonald, Shari
PN6231 .R4 L66 2003
818' .60208 — dc21
                                                    2002155410

All Scripture quotations, unless otherwise indicated, are taken from the *Holy Bible, New International Version*®. NIV®. Copyright © 1973, 1978, 1984 by International Bible Society. Used by permission of Zondervan. All rights reserved.

Interior design by Tracey Moran

Printed in the United States of America

---

04 05 06 07 08 09 /❖ DC/ 10 9 8

Contents

Preface

William Makepeace Thackeray, a Victorian novelist, once wrote that "a good laugh is sunshine in a house." We hope that *Look Who's Laughing!* will not only add sunshine to your home but to your heart as well, easing your anxieties, giving much-needed perspective, and lightening whatever loads you might be carrying.

As we worked on the project over the past year, Shari and I have encountered our share of challenges in other aspects of our lives. But evening after evening as I set aside the pressures of the day and worked on the collection of material that eventually made its way into the pages of this book, I felt the pressure ease and slip away. Instead of ending the day worried or frustrated, I often slipped into bed with a smile on my face and a settled peace in my heart.

As you read through the stories, quips, and quotes in this book, we hope that you too will experience laughter's power to refresh and renew your soul, restoring a sense of balance regardless of life's difficulties.

We are grateful to the many people who have made this book possible, especially to the authors whose work it includes. Their ability to see the fun and funny side of life and their candidness about their own foibles and failings helps all of us to learn and relearn one of life's most important skills—the art of laughing at ourselves and our circumstances. Thanks also to the many publishers who kindly gave permission for use of the material in this book.

Particular thanks goes to Sandy VanderZicht, executive editor at Zondervan, who is also the editor of the two previous books in the series: *She Who Laughs, Lasts!* and *Don't Stop Laughing Now!* Sandy is a woman who laughs easily and heartily (even at my none-too-funny jokes) and who is quick to appreciate and enjoy the humorous side of life. Her guidance has been invaluable as we have worked on questions of content and structure, hoping thereby to tickle as many funny bones as possible.

We also want to acknowledge Dirk Buursma, our development editor, whose prayers and encouragement are greatly appreciated. Thanks also to Sue Brower, director of marketing for trade books. Sue and her creative team have energetically supported this book as well as its predecessors, making it their mission to spread the laughter as far and wide as possible.

To you, the reader, we hope for many days of lighthearted fun and ample joy as you read through the pages of *Look Who's Laughing!* You might even try, as I did, reading a few pages before bedtime and then tucking yourself in with a smile, experiencing the truth of the biblical saying that "a merry heart doeth good like a medicine."

—Ann Spangler

CHAPTER ONE

Men Are Funny, Women Are Hilarious . . . Together We're Hysterical

Man is the powder, woman the spark.
—Lope De Vega

Women like silent men.
They think they are listening.
—Marcel Achard

One Man's Treasure

G. Ron Darbee

I suppose I should have seen it coming, should have recognized the signs, picked up on the subtle hint. But after so many years of marriage, I really didn't want to believe it was true. Oh, she sent all the right signals, I guess. She even threatened a time or two. Maybe I loved her too much, trusted her too completely. When it finally happened—when all that trust shattered and her veil of secrecy lifted—there was no one left to blame but myself.

I went to bed early, consistent with my usual routine, but rather than falling directly to sleep, I waited. Because of my morning commute, it's not unusual for me to retire before Sue, anyway. I didn't think she knew of my suspicions, but later she claimed she did. In a way, I think she wanted to be caught, to get it out in the open and end the sneaking around.

About an hour later, Sue poked her head in the door, ensuring herself I was out for the night. I heard the fumbling of keys in her purse and the sound of the back door creaking before I rose and followed in pursuit. Stepping into the garage behind her, I caught her red-handed.

"Ah!" I said, in the manner of one who has just caught his spouse red-handed. "So what do you have to say for yourself?"

Sue spun around quickly, startled and caught off guard. Following her first impulse, she feigned surprise and pretended to gasp for breath, all the while attempting to hide something in the small of her back. I didn't fall for the clever ruse and demanded to see what she held behind her.

"It's nothing," Sue said. "Really . . . nothing." Her face displayed only guilt, and shame shone through the facade of shock.

"Nothing, is it?" I said. "We'll see about that. What have you got there? What are you hiding behind your back?"

"Don't make me show you," she pleaded. "Please, can we just go inside and forget about this? Pretend it never happened?"

"I don't think so, Sue. It's gone too far. I'll be seeing what you're hiding there now, if you please."

Slowly, cautiously, she pulled her hand around. I knew what to expect even before I saw it. "Those are my baseball cards, aren't they?" I said, my heart nearly pounding through my chest. "You've been cleaning out the garage again, haven't you?"

"Yes!" She said it defiantly, holding her head up high, ready to stand her ground. She had done it, yes, and she was glad.

"And you've been rummaging through my things?" I asked. "I suppose you've thrown away some of my stuff?"

"Yes," she answered, "and I'd do it again if I had the chance. It's all junk. Somebody had to clear it out of here."

So there it was, a turning point, a roadblock in our marriage. We could take the easy way, like so many other couples we knew, or we could try to work it out. Our life together was too important to both of us; we had made a commitment, a lifelong commitment.

"We can work this out, sweetheart," I said, in the spirit of reconciliation. "Let me see it all. We'll do this thing together."

That was one of the most difficult things I have ever done. Sue, like many women, doesn't know the first thing about memorabilia. She sees a box of baseball cards, an old ball glove—and immediately heads toward the trash pile. And the whole time our house is cluttered with real junk: photographs, old letters, and hand-me-downs disguised as family heirlooms.

"Show me what you've thrown away so far," I said, wanting to minimize the losses. She pointed toward a trash can nearly overflowing with my possessions. "Not my first ball glove!" I yelled as I extracted the crown of my earthly treasures. "You couldn't have meant to throw away my baseball mitt."

"It doesn't even fit you anymore," Sue said. "You couldn't possibly get your hand in there."

"But it has Ron Swoboda's signature on the thumb, Sue! How could you do this?"

"I don't see a signature on it," she said, squinting in the poor light of our garage.

"Well, it used to be on there," I said. "You can sort of make it out if you know what to look for." I continued rummaging through the pile. "Now wait just a minute. Do you know what this is?" I asked. "Do you know what you've thrown away?"

"Old baseball cards," Sue said. Accurate guess, but she obviously didn't get the whole picture.

"Not just old baseball cards, Sue. This is Mickey Mantle, 'Mick the Stick,' one of the greatest baseball players of all time. Do you know how much this is worth? I'll tell you. Several hundred dollars!"

"I apologize," Sue said. "I never would have thrown it away if I'd known how much it was worth. Can we sell it?"

"Sell it! This is my youth we're talking about, Sue. How much is my youth worth to you?"

"How much can we get?" she asked.

Determining that we were getting nowhere following that course, I switched gears slightly and attempted to gain the upper hand. "How much of *your* junk have you thrown away, sweetheart?" I asked.

"Over there by the shelves," she pointed in the direction of the washing machine. "A toilet brush that's seen better days, some slippers, and that cookbook your mother gave me."

I couldn't believe my ears. "The cookbook my mother wrote with her own two hands?" I asked. "You threw away Mom's Chronology of Darbee Cuisine? How could you?"

"It's not even a real cookbook, just a list of ingredients," Sue argued. "She didn't write down any amounts. What am I supposed to do—guess?"

"Okay, fine," I said. "Why are we saving this then?" I picked up an old encyclopedia volume and thrust it in Sue's direction. "Open the book, Sue, and you know what you'll find? Dead flowers. May I ask why we are saving dead flowers?"

"Those happen to be the first flowers you sent me," Sue said, as though that revelation was supposed to make a difference.

"They're still dead, Sue," I said. "And, quite frankly, I don't understand. Mickey you toss away without a second thought, and a dozen carnations get immortalized between the pages of World Book."

"Roses," she corrected. "They were roses, and I thought it was better to save them than expect new ones on occasion."

Immediately recognizing that this, too, was not a course I wanted to take, I changed directions one last time. "Sounds like we compromise," I said. "I'll tell you what, I don't mind if you keep the dried flowers. How's that?"

"Fine," she said, "and you can keep Sticky Mickey if it means that much to you."

"Mick the Stick, honey," I corrected. "Yes, it means that much to me. Why don't we try to get through the rest of this stuff tomorrow after we've both gotten some sleep. We'll get a fresh start."

"Okay, and I'm sorry I tossed your things without first considering your feelings."

We headed for the bedroom, hand in hand, the disagreement now behind us, when Sue asked another question. "By the way," she said, "what was the tooth you saved in the baby food jar?"

"Tell me you didn't throw away the tooth," I said. "That wasn't just any tooth, Sue. That tooth belonged to Dave Schultze, hatchet man for the Philadelphia Flyers back in the seventies. I picked it up off the ice after an Islanders game. At least I think it belonged to Schultze. Hockey players lose a lot of teeth, and it's not always easy keeping track *and* watching the puck, too."

"You took the man's tooth?" Sue asked in a voice that suggested disbelief. "Didn't you offer to give it back to him at least?"

"Nah," I said. "Those guys drop their teeth all the time. They're like souvenirs. If they really cared about their dental work, they wouldn't be playing ice hockey, now would they?"

"I guess not, but I still think you should have at least offered," she said. "And, by the way, the tooth goes."

"Let's talk about it in the morning, sweetheart."

"The tooth goes."

"Goodnight, Sue," I said.

"Goodnight."

As we drifted off to sleep, I thought about how some people can't seem to appreciate the finer, more sentimental things in life. And for all this time I had lived under the impression that women were the more emotional partners. It's just lucky she didn't find my collection of athletic footwear. I'm sure she would have burned them.

Light His Fire

Becky Freeman

I am not, by any stretch of the imagination, what you would call a naturally wild and wanton woman. But I'd been married fifteen years, and I felt our marriage needed a little—spice.

It all began with a romantic suggestion I gleaned from a book titled *Light His Fire*. The author, Ellen Kriedman, suggests that wives use their ingenuity to come up with imaginative ways to have fun seducing their mate. The book assured me that, done properly, this technique should fire up the "I feel a chill in the air" times most couples experience at some point in their relationship.

Nothing new here, really. Ever since the days when perky Mrs. Marabel Morgan first suggested we Christian women greet our husbands at the door dressed in plastic wrap and/or an apron, we wives have spent a couple of decades trying to outdo the Total Woman. Personally, I have come to the conclusion that such efforts leave me feeling more like a Totaled Woman. Not that I hadn't given wild and creative tactics my best shot, mind you.

One night as I stepped out of the shower wrapped in a towel, I spied the lights of Scott's pickup in the driveway of our home. Our closest neighbors were raccoons and possums, so I didn't worry about the undraped window overlooking the drive. Suddenly I could almost hear Dr. Kriedman whispering in my ear. *Why not? After all, you're married to the guy. Be playful! Be sexy! Have some fun with your man!*

So I dropped the towel and stood there in front of the window wearing nothing but my best seductive smile. As it happened, Scott was not alone. This night he had with him our good friend Gary, husband of my dear friend Mary. As the two men walked casually toward the house (I learned later), Scott glanced toward the window, returned for a second to his conversation with Gary, and then jerked his head back toward the window, his eyes wide, his mouth agape. He then alternated between trying to divert Gary's eyes from our bedroom window and gesturing frantically for me to run for cover.

Lamentably, although it is easy to see *into* a lighted home from the dark, it is quite difficult for the one standing inside the house to see *out* into the dark. Because of this phenomenon, I imagined Scott must surely be whooping it up out there in the night air. I even thought I heard him egging me on with playful wolf whistles. Later I would discover the "whistles" were actually high-pitched sounds made by Scott's vocal chords desperately searching for the natural range of his voice. In any case, I simply responded to what I had assumed was my husband's enthusiastic reaction.

Finally, having safely escorted Gary into the kitchen, Scott breathed a sigh of relief and began to relax. Observing that nothing could undo the damage that had already been done, my husband nonchalantly poked his head into the bedroom.

"Hi, hon," he said casually. "Gary's with me."

My screams, I'm sure, awakened every possum and raccoon in the surrounding square mile. I thought I would die. My thoughts were frenzied. *I've* just flashed my best friend's husband! It doesn't get any worse than this. Of all the stupid antics—this absolutely tops the list! I vowed to avoid Gary for the rest of my life. I couldn't possibly face him again without dissolving into a puddle of shame and embarrassment.

The next morning, Mary—Gary's wife—called bright and early. "Becky," she said brightly, "Gary asked me to deliver a message to you." Switching to a deep French accent, she went on. "He says to tell you, 'Becky, jou look mahvalhlous.'"

When the laughter finally began to subside on her end of the line, Mary added, "And, hey, I just want you to know, since I've been feeling a bit under the weather lately, this probably *made* his week."

Because they both had a great sense of humor, we all recovered fairly quickly. With time and understanding, I am now able to hold a normal conversation with Gary without benefit of a paper bag over my head.

The Window Story has already made its way through our small town—down grocery store aisles, across neighborhood fences, into most of our fellow parishioners' ears between services—and is probably being translated into several foreign languages. My best friends, and even my husband, love to tell it at appropriate gatherings when conversation hits a lull.

After that little escapade, one would assume I would have laid to rest any impulse to do something wild and crazy and romantic— for at least a while. One would assume.

Then one evening, feeling rather amorous, I stepped out of the bathtub and noticed a large, yellow, transparent bag hanging over the towel rack—a bag that had been used to cover Scott's dry-cleaned shirts. Viewing all that plastic, I thought I heard voices again. This time it was the Total Woman speaking. *If at first you don't succeed, try, try again.*

Inspired, I draped the mustard-colored wrap around my torso, ingeniously holding it together with a couple of bobby pins I had found in the sink. Slinking toward the bedroom where my husband was reclining with a good book, I opened the door with a flourish. He continued to read, so I loudly cleared my throat. He finally glanced up, shook his head as if to clear it, frowned in bewilderment, and scratched his chin. Not quite the reaction I had anticipated. It got worse.

"What have you done to yourself now?" Scott asked sincerely. "You've made your entire body look like one of those supermarket meat trays of pickled pigs' feet!"

I wasn't as crushed as you might expect from that verbal blow to my ego. I had to admit, a last-minute glance in the bathroom mirror had filled me with a few serious doubts. I had gone into this mission knowing its outcome was chancy at best. But I was no longer in a wild and crazy romantic state of mind either. As to my pork-minded husband's chances for an evening of love, I have just one thing to say—"That little piggy had none."

Egg Money

Anonymous

The elderly pastor was searching his closet for his collar before church one Sunday morning. In the back of the closet, he found a small box containing three eggs and one hundred $1 bills. He called his wife into the closet to ask her about the box and its contents.

Embarrassed, she admitted having hidden the box there for their entire forty-five years of marriage. Disappointed and hurt, the pastor asked her, "Why!?" The wife replied that she hadn't wanted to hurt his feelings.

He asked her how the box could possibly have hurt his feelings. She said that every time he had delivered a poor sermon, she had placed an egg in the box.

The pastor felt that three poor sermons in forty-five years was certainly nothing to feel bad about, so he asked her what the $100 was for.

She replied, "Each time I got a dozen eggs, I sold them to the neighbors for a dollar."

Pearly Gates

John Ortberg

A man appears before the pearly gates.

"Have you ever done anything of particular merit?" Saint Peter asks.

"Well, I can think of one thing," the man offers. "Once I came upon a gang of high-testosterone bikers who were threatening a young woman. I directed them to leave her alone, but they wouldn't listen. So I approached the largest and most heavily tattooed biker. I smacked him on the head, kicked his bike over, ripped out his nose ring and threw it on the ground, and told him, 'Leave her alone now, or you'll answer to me.'"

Saint Peter was impressed. "When did this happen?"

"A couple of minutes ago."

Pause for Concern

Dave Meurer

Solve the Mystery: An ill-fated family of four is stranded in a car on a country road in South Dakota during the worst blizzard of the century. One person has numb toes, one person's teeth are chattering, one person is shivering, and one person is fanning herself and saying, "Gracious, it is so *hot* in here."

> QUESTION: Which one is experiencing menopause?
> HINT: If you answer correctly, you may get whacked with a
>   spatula.

I had never even heard the word *menopause* when it decided to pay my mom a nice little visit (in the sense that a forest fire pays Yellowstone a nice little visit). I came home from school one day and walked in the door and said, "Hi, Mom," and she erupted in a geyser of tears, collapsed on the sofa, and sobbed, "Go ahead, just rub it in!"

I turned quizzically to my dad, who was wildly making the universal gesture for "Meet Me in Ohio!"

Dad drove me across four county lines before he cleared his throat and announced, "Your mother is going through 'The Change.'"

"The change of what?" I asked.

Dad bit his lip.

"Son, there comes a time in every woman's life when her body decides that her childbearing days are over. Her hormones are in a state of upheaval, and it is exhibited in moodiness, hot flashes, tears, and the ability to rip the doors off a Brinks armored truck if chocolate is inside. Just try to be understanding."

That directive turned out to be easier said than done.

The term "try to be understanding" implies that there is something that can, in fact, be understood—like algebra or mathematical word problems, which at least involve logic. Menopause is more complex than quantum physics, and no rules of logic apply ...

Although it will still be several years before The Change descends on our house, the Meurer household is already in training for this momentous event. We hold monthly drills called PMS, which is sort of like training for a National Guard exercise except that it's more dangerous and we don't even get free uniforms.

Women believe it is tremendously unfair that they have to endure PMS, childbirth, *and* menopause, because they think men pretty much get off scot-free. But they are mistaken. While it is true that women have to do the labor thing and the childbirth thing, and endure the cramps, aches, pains, water retention, bloating, hot flashes, sudden fits of weeping, hormone-driven maniacal mood swings, and embarrassing OB/GYN exams, they need to bear in mind that guys have to *live in the same house with them* while all this is happening. So we males are certainly shouldering our share of the suffering. Hey, I think you could even argue that guys are doing *most* of the heavy lifting, because sometimes we even have to go to the store late at night to buy Midol for our women folk.

WHACK, WHACK, WHACK!!! OW, OW, OW!!!

You may recall that in the biblical account wherein God told Abraham that the pitter-patter of little feet would soon be heard around the tent, Sarah, who was nearly one hundred years old, laughed. While the text tells us it was a laugh of unbelief, we can conjecture that one component of this unbelief may have taken the form of Sarah thinking to herself, "Surely, *the Lord would not make me go through menopause TWICE?!? I can't* believe *it!*"

Be that as it may, the happy couple did get a baby out of the ordeal—it's just that half of the happy couple was a bit happier than the other and had less stretch marks.

But it is all a package deal. The entire PMS/pregnancy/menopause thing is a wondrously orchestrated system God has created so that we can bring children into the world to nurture and teach and then release into adulthood to start the amazing process all over again—with menopause serving as an "off switch" so that women finally get a break and do not have kids at the age of one hundred unless God is really trying to make a major point.

Although we don't understand why much of this has to be kind of an unpleasant experience for women, we need to trust that, in the grace and goodness of God, there is, in fact, a reason for it. At minimum, we can be thankful that, except for those late-night Midol runs, men pretty much get to skate. Works for me!

WHACK, WHACK, WHACK!!! OW, OW, OW!!!

Showdown at the Hoedown

Becky Freeman

*U*nder normal circumstances my husband can gracefully tolerate any number of my faults. I can back over multiple mailboxes, get stuck in ditches, leave my purse in out-of-town restaurants, and forget to mail important checks, yet all is quickly forgiven.

But in our earlier married life there was one thing my husband had never been able to tolerate, not even for a second, and that was for me to be in a negative mood. His attitude was, *Get over it and get over it yesterday.* Here was an area in our marriage where I had come to feel I wasn't being given any slack in the ol' fishing line—no leeway to express even one moment of plain old everyday grumpiness. Once every month we added my drop in hormones to Scott's lack of tolerance, and we had an explosion just waiting to happen. Unfortunately, one time happened to coincide with my birthday.

Scott and I were driving to Dallas, Texas, to meet my parents at a country-western family steak house—The Trail Dust—to celebrate. The Trail Dust had long been a family favorite; it had a wonderful band and was one of the few wholesome places where we could go to two-step, waltz, or dance the Cotton-Eyed Joe. Mother and Daddy were getting to be quite the fancy country-western dancers, and we had always enjoyed each other's company, so we were looking forward to the evening out with them.

As we were driving I mulled over the variety of special occasions we'd celebrated at this steak house over the years—Scott's graduation from college, numerous birthdays, and a couple of anniversaries. Then, however, I recalled a couple of special celebrations that had been a little hard on my ego. On my thirtieth birthday, for example, the bandleader had coerced me into coming up to the front, donning a white cowboy hat, and galloping around the dance floor on a stick horse while the packed-out restaurant sang "Happy Birthday to You." Now isn't that special? I was stuck in one of those classic unavoidable dilemmas. If I declined to trot around the floor like an overgrown child on a stick horse, I would have looked like a spoilsport. If I accepted the invitation, I would look like an idiot. Better to be an Idiot than a Party Pooper, so I pranced proudly with my head held high and my dignity still somewhat intact.

But I remembered yet another celebration dinner at the Trail Dust that had pretty much stripped me of any remaining vestiges of pride. That evening, Scott and I had been seated across the table from some rather dignified young men from our church—one was an engineer, the other a physician. To this day I don't know how it happened, because I had certainly not been drinking anything stronger than root beer, but as I was debating a serious point, I became airborne and somehow fell straight back in my chair and onto the floor. There I sat in my ladder-back chair, staring at the *ceiling* instead of across the table at the two young men.

Of course I was wearing a dress. Of course I landed with my boots sticking straight up in the air. As nonchalantly as he might have reached for a fallen set of keys, Scott scooped me up and, without a word, set me back in the upright position. Didn't lose a beat. Just propped me up like a rag doll and went right on with his meal and conversation. The two gentlemen, as I recall, sat poised with forks in midair, blinking as if to be sure of what they had just seen.

As we drove toward my birthday celebration, I recalled these past events and felt suddenly uneasy about another Trail Dust celebration. As Scott and I neared the halfway point on the highway to the familiar steak house, my general uneasiness turned to strong irritation, coupled with a sudden high-dosage bolt of low self-esteem, and things went downhill from there.

"So why don't you like my dress, Scott?" I began.

"I didn't say I didn't like your dress!"

"Well, you didn't say you *did,* either. And you didn't say I looked pretty tonight. You always tell me I look ravishing when we go out. What is it? Do I look heavy? Are you embarrassed to have me as your partner?"

"I'm not going to have this conversation, Becky."

"You are talking to me, so you *are* having this conversation."

Silence followed for the next thirty minutes. I guessed maybe we *weren't* having this conversation after all. When we pulled into the restaurant parking lot, I could stand it no longer.

"I can't believe you ruined my birthday dinner by refusing to tell me I look ravishing!"

Then I flounced out of the truck, slammed the door hard enough to loosen every tooth in his head, and marched into the steak house. I was pretty sure Scott would follow me, even though my behavior surely wasn't all that ravishing. After all, it was my birthday, and we were meeting my parents, for goodness sake. But did I mention that my husband has a wee stubborn streak?

I walked into the restaurant and glanced back over my shoulder, expecting to see a properly penitent husband trailing just behind. There was a huge empty space instead. So I made up a plausible excuse to tell my parents. I told them that Scott had probably gone to get some gas and would be right back, all the while inwardly hoping that what I said would turn out to be the truth. I kept a sharp eye peeled for him—even praying that he would walk through those swinging doors any minute and bring the standoff to an end. But no sign of my tall husband graced the entry. After about twenty minutes I ran out of excuses. We were into a standoff to rival the one at the O.K. Corral. But no longer up to a shootout, I began to cry into my iced tea.

Not knowing what else to do, Daddy asked me if I would like to dance, and I managed to nod. So I "Waltzed Across Texas" in my father's arms while the tears poured down my cheeks over the fact that my birthday dinner had been ruined, that my husband was behaving like a stubborn mule sitting out in the parking lot, and, most of all, that I was not ravishing tonight.

Finally, I told my parents that Scott and I had had a little tiff on the way to the restaurant. They both managed to feign surprise and registered the appropriate sympathy for me. Then I told them that if they would excuse me I had to go out to the parking lot to apologize to my hardheaded, insensitive husband.

I found Scott sitting in the truck, his hard head resting against the steering wheel. As soon as I opened the door, Scott took a good look at my tearstained face. "Becky," he said grimly, "what time of the month is it?"

How *like* a man—so totally irrational!

"It's my birthday. That's what time of the month it is! Did you know that it is my *birthday?* How can you stand me up on my *birthday?* And in front of my *parents!*"

"Becky, I'm sorry," he said, shaking his head as if to clear it. "I just don't know what to *do* with you. You're like a different person when you hit a certain time of the month. You hate yourself. And you try your best to pick a fight with me. And it works every time! You've got to do something!"

I felt tremendous relief that he wasn't going to leave me stranded there and began to hope that the evening could be salvaged. I even toyed with the remote possibility he might be a tiny bit right.

"Well," I said, sniffing and trying to smile, "I'll make you a deal. I'll see a doctor soon if you'll come inside and do the Cotton-Eyed Joe with me."

When we walked inside the restaurant to our table arm in arm, Mother shook her head and grinned.

"You know, you two are a lot of trouble—but you're never more trouble than you're worth. Let's eat!"

We made it through the evening—and even managed to have a good time. Once as I waltzed in my husband's arms, he stopped and whispered in my ear something that I desperately needed to hear.

"Miss Becky, you look ravishing tonight."

A Day at the Beach

Chonda Pierce

There's nothing like a late-night telephone call from the local police department to shake up your day.

My best friend, Alison, owns a place near Charleston, South Carolina, just off the coast. For the last several years I've gone there for at least a week to do nothing but eat, sleep, shop, and shop. For me, it's a place to park my brain and to replace all the city air in my lungs with ocean air.

But this particular year, late at night, while Alison and I were in a heated battle of Rummikub (only the greatest board game ever invented), the phone rang. Alison's son, Justin, answered. After a short moment all the blood drained from his face, and we heard him say, "You'd better talk to my momma." Alison took the phone and held it so we could both hear.

"Sorry to bother you so late tonight, ma'am," the nasal voice said. "My name is Sergeant Lipton, and I'm just making a few routine calls to residents of the community to say we believe we're close to an arrest of Crazy Eddie."

"Crazy Eddie?"

"Yes, ma'am. If you've been listening to the news, you're probably aware of his escape earlier in the day. We've been all over this island with dogs and cops and soldiers and swamp buggies. And now—"

"So he's still loose?" Alison interrupted. Her husband was working two hundred miles away, and my husband, David, wasn't supposed to fly in until the next day. So there we were in a tiny beach house, Alison and me, with three children and a crazy man who had just escaped from prison and had somehow outrun a swamp buggy.

"Well, he's sort of loose," said Sergeant Lipton.

"Sort of loose? How can he be sort of loose?" said Alison.

"Because it's late, and he's probably exhausted after wrestling the gators and—"

"What are you talking about?"

"Well, we had him cornered in a swamp on the island's southeast side, and a gator jumped him and—"

"And what?"

"And he killed the gator and got away."

"He what?"

"But like I said, we're really close to an arrest."

"How can you be so sure?" I hollered into the receiver.

"Because we've cornered him at the Seaside Mall," Sergeant Lipton continued and then paused, as Alison and I wondered what that had to do with anything. "And if I've done my homework right, ma'am," he added, "one good mall—no matter what part of the country it's in—can literally suck the life out of any man, no matter how strong or how crazy he might be."

Something clicked inside my head, and I took the receiver from Alison, who had also turned very pale by now. "David, is that you?" I asked.

Sergeant Lipton—Crazy Eddie . . . David began to cackle on the other end.

"That's *not* funny," I told him. "It's David," I said to Alison, and the blood began to return to her face, faster than was probably healthy.

"I'm going to kill him," she said, not caring how many witnesses overheard.

"Just settle down, Alison," I told her after I'd finished "speaking" with David and hung up the phone. "Besides, he won't be here until tomorrow."

David came in late the next day and couldn't wait to go down to the beach. Alison and I had cooled down a bit, but we still made David carry the cooler, the towels, and all the beach toys for the two-block walk.

"I can't believe you guys fell for that," said David, as he tottered barefoot down the drive, arms full of beach stuff. Alison and I didn't say a word, trying not to encourage him. "I mean, Sergeant Lipton! I made up the name from a tea box right there on the spot."

Hahahahahahahahaha!

Just before we reached the end of the drive I heard Alison say, "You know, you might want to wear some sandals. It's been very hot, and the road might be—"

"Ouch! Ouch!" David whooped as he danced around in a tiny circle. The cooler lid flopped open and closed, all the beach towels slid to the ground, plastic shovels and buckets flew off to the right and left. "Hot! Hot! Hot!" he yelled. On his tiptoes, trying to find a way off the hot pavement, he made a beeline for the skinny grassy island in the median.

Again I heard Alison say, just before he got there, "Watch out for the sandspurs!"

But David had already hopped onto the sandy, grassy patch and, for just a second, seemed to find relief. His peaceful expression didn't last long though, before his face twisted into the most painful expression I'd ever seen. He raised one foot and lowered it and then raised the other, as though he were climbing invisible stairs. Whenever he would lift up a foot, we could see all sorts of sticks and grass and prickly things stuck to the bottom—stuff he couldn't shake off.

Sandspurs!

I'm not sure who started to laugh first. It may have been me, or Alison, or perhaps even the children. All I know is that we were laughing so hard we could barely stand up. I couldn't catch my breath. Tears began to flow down Alison's face. The children were hopping around like David—cackling and laughing. Alison managed to pull her video camera from its bag and start to shoot, but the video is so bouncy it's hard to watch.

David lay on his back on the hot pavement and stuck both feet straight up in the air. The bottoms of them were covered with the prickly, green sandspurs.

Alison finally came to the rescue and made him roll over onto one of the big beach towels. (This is where the video begins to steady somewhat, and we can get a better look at all the sandspurs in the bottoms of his feet.)

That day convinced me that God is still working on me (and Alison), because—after a bit—both of us began to pick off the little prickly things from the bottoms of David's feet and toss the stickers to the side. David just lay there in the middle of the drive, legs raised high and feet swaying back and forth in the breeze that blew in from the ocean (we never made it there that day), repeating, "Ouch, that hurts. Ouch, that hurts."

"Okay, Sergeant Lipton," Alison said. "This will probably hurt a little—but not as much as wrestling gators."

Pluck. Pluck. Pluck.

After several long minutes, we helped David hobble back to the house. We split up the towels and toys between the kids, and Alison and I carried the cooler back home.

Weeks later I finally sorted out what happened. (Before that, every time I'd get close, I'd start to laugh, and that's as far as I could get.) Eventually I could see God's mercy playing out that day. I realized that, no matter how much we'd like to see someone get what's coming to him, there's always a place for compassion—for mercy. No matter how much David had frightened us the night before, it was right for us to help him when he needed us.

Now, I think Alison may still have some sorting out to do. When I asked her what she learned from the experience, she simply said, "That God can use even lowly sandspurs to dole out justice on his people when they stray."

Give it time. I believe she's still a bit upset with Sergeant Lipton.

The Offering

Anonymous

*O*ne Sunday a pastor told his congregation that the church needed some extra money and asked the people to prayerfully consider putting a little extra in the offering plate. He said that whoever gave the most would be able to pick out three hymns.

After the offering plates were passed, the pastor glanced down and noticed that someone had placed a $1,000 bill in the offering. He was so excited that he immediately shared his joy with his congregation and said he'd like to personally thank the person who placed the money in the plate.

Rosie, from all the way in the back, shyly raised her hand. The pastor asked her to come to the front. Slowly she made her way to the pastor. He told her how wonderful it was that she gave so much, and in thanksgiving he asked her to pick out three hymns.

Her eyes brightened as she looked over the congregation, pointed to the three most handsome men in the building, and said, "I'll take him and him and him."

Slapstick

Becky Freeman

Just when I think my life is growing dull and I'm running out of material, something seems to fall in my lap from out of nowhere.

It's a laid-back Sunday evening. Or at least it was. The family seemed content, and all of them looked happily occupied. Some were sprawled on the living room couch watching a movie, one was soaking in the bathtub, another was reading a book. So I thought I'd sneak off for a few minutes to work on this manuscript.

Suddenly the body of a large man fell against the door, knocking it open as he collapsed at my feet. I recognized him as my husband. He had contracted into a fetal position, holding both legs against his chest. As I helped him to the couch, he winced—and through his clenched teeth I understood him to say, "You'll never believe what I did."

"Oh? What makes you think I wouldn't believe it, baby?"

I cautiously untied his shoes and helped him out of his jeans. At this point he began to see the humor in the situation. He was laughing and moaning at the same time. I could see a large scratch across one thigh—and whatever it was that had given him the scratch had also torn through his jeans in the process. On the other leg, a large goose egg was already beginning to swell on his right kneecap. It hurt to look at it. I ran into the kitchen for ice and asked Zeke to help me move his dad into the living room, where I gave him a couple of pills for his pain.

Once we were able to assess my husband's wounds and determine that nothing was broken, I asked for details. "So would you like to talk about it now?"

"Well, it's really embarrassing," he said.

I thought of all the dangerous situations my husband had put himself in as he worked on our house every weekend—wiring high-voltage electrical circuits, lifting heavy beams, operating circular saws from lofty perches, and, of course, hanging from the rafters by one hand with a caulk gun in the other. I thought to myself, *Nothing my husband did to injure himself would surprise me.*

I was wrong.

"Come on, Scott," I probed. "I promise I won't yell at you. What did you do this time? Were you trying to move that table saw without asking for help? Did you fall between the beams? Did the truck trailer collapse on you? What?"

He grinned sheepishly. "Remember that metal workbench I moved from the neighbor's house to our backyard today? Let's just say that while I was running around in the dark, I found it."

"Should I ask why you were running outside in the dark?"

"Maybe that wouldn't be such a good idea."

"Come on, I can't stand the suspense. Tell me."

"Well, you know how our septic system has been overloaded with all the rain we've been having? So I thought I'd be frugal and go outside behind a tree in the dark, and—well, you know. I'd just finished two large glasses of iced tea, so I guess I was in a hurry to get to the woods. That's when I ran into the workbench and turned a flip into the night air."

So collapsed was I with laughter that I laid my head on Scott's shoulder and wiped the tears away. He was in the same condition, though every time he laughed it also brought on a moan.

"So, Scott," I gasped, "what you're trying to tell me is that you nearly broke both legs trying to ... "

"Yes. Are you satisfied now?"

"Yes, I am. I really am. Scott?"

"What?"

"Can I use this?"

"What do you mean?"

"Can I write about it?"

"Becky, you're like a vulture circling weakened prey. Every time anybody does anything stupid, there you are, like Lois Lane with her pad and pencil. Am I nothing but *material* to you?" But even as he said it he was laughing, so I felt pretty sure I was close to getting the go-ahead.

"Oh, Scott, you know I love you with all my heart, and I am so sorry you are in pain. But how could you question my motives? Didn't I just give you my very own pain medication a few minutes ago?"

"What pain medication? I thought you gave me some Tylenol."

"Well, we're out of Tylenol. So I gave you some of my Midol PMS multi-symptom relief tablets."

"What??? You gave me girl pills!?"

"See how cranky you are? You needed those pills. You'll feel much better in a few minutes."

"What do those things do?"

"Well, they keep you from fussing at those who love you."

"Is that so? And how?"

"They make you go to sleep and render you incapable of communication."

"Hmmm—well, I *am* feeling kind of drowsy." His eyelids began to droop.

I waited a few more minutes before I spoke again.

"So it's okay with you, honey, after you drift off to sleep and everything, if I go back out to my office and write about this?"

"Um ... what? ... I'm so tired ... whatev ... "

"I'll take that as a yes," I said, and dashed for the computer.

It's now the morning after the "accident." I rolled over in bed about 6:30 A.M. and woke my husband from his peaceful slumber by seductively wrapping my leg around his swollen knee. Honestly—I forgot! Once he stopped shrieking, he managed to get dressed for work. As he hobbled around in his pitiful condition, I asked him, "So, Scott, what are you going to tell the gals at work this morning about how you got your limp?"

"I'll say it was a skiing accident. Or maybe I got sideswiped by a truck. Which story do you think sounds more manly?"

"Well, don't worry," I answered, batting my eyelashes. "Your little secret is safe with me."

"Suuure it is. I'll proofread the chapter tonight."

It is now the *day after* "The Day after the Accident." A few hours ago, as I was putting my makeup on in the bathroom, the body of a large man fell against the bathroom door, knocking it open as he fell to the floor. Guess who? Same song, second verse. He was once again holding his knee and curled up in the fetal position.

"Oh, Scott," I said as I helped him sit up, "what have you done now?"

"Well, it's embarrassing," he moaned, gingerly examining his wound.

"It's broad daylight. Please tell me you weren't looking for a tree—"

"No, no, no. It wasn't that bad. This time I just whacked my leg with a two-by-four."

"Hold on a second. Don't say another word. You hop in the tub and soak your knee while I run to get a pad and pencil."

I was back in a flash.

"OK, Scott. Now tell me again what happened, and don't leave out any details."

"Well, there's not much to tell, really. I was trying to get the porch post aligned, so I picked up a two-by-four and gave the post a few hard whacks—only on one of the backswings I whacked my sore leg."

My husband seems to be stuck in a painful slapstick comedy routine. And here he was, *literally,* slapping himself with a stick. I am truly sorry he's in pain, but you have to admit, he's been entertaining.

Some days it's really a lot of fun to be married.

CHAPTER TWO

Just for Laughs

*No man [or woman] who has once heartily
and wholly laughed can be
altogether irreclaimably bad.*
–Thomas Carlyle

*Laughter is a tranquilizer
with no side effects.*
–Arnold Glasgow

Insurance Claims

Anonymous

The following are actual statements found on insurance forms, where drivers attempted to summarize the details of an accident in the fewest words possible:

- I thought my window was down but found it was up when I put my head through it.
- The other car collided with mine without warning of its intention.
- The guy was all over the road. I had to swerve a number of times before I hit him.
- I pulled away from the side of the road, glanced at my mother-in-law, and headed over the embankment.
- In my attempt to kill a fly, I drove into a telephone pole.
- I had been driving for forty years when I fell asleep at the wheel and had an accident.
- I was on my way to the doctor with rear-end trouble when my universal joint gave way, causing me to have an accident.
- The pedestrian had no idea which direction to run, so I ran over him.
- The indirect cause of the accident was a little guy in a small car with a big mouth.

Takeoffs and Landings

Anonymous

Occasionally, airline attendants endeavor to make the "in-flight safety lecture" a bit more entertaining. Here are some real examples that have been heard or reported:

- "There may be fifty ways to leave your lover, but there are only four ways out of this airplane."
- "Your seat cushions can be used for flotation, and in the event of an emergency water landing, please take them with our compliments."
- "Smoking in the lavatories is prohibited. Any person caught smoking in the lavatories will be asked to leave the plane immediately."
- This is an actual joke heard on Southwest Airlines just after a very hard landing in Salt Lake City, Utah—one of the most bone jarring ever experienced. The flight attendant came on the intercom and said, "That was quite a bump, and I know what y'all are thinking. I'm here to tell you it wasn't the airline's fault, it wasn't the pilot's fault, it wasn't the flight attendant's fault—it was the asphalt!"
- An airline pilot wrote that on this particular flight he had hammered his ship into the runway really hard. The airline had a policy that required the first officer to stand at the door as the passengers exited and to give a smile and a "thanks for flying XYZ Airline." He said that, in light of his bad landing, he had a hard time looking the passengers in

the eye, thinking that someone would have a smart comment. Finally everyone had gotten off except for a little old lady walking with a cane. She said, "Sonny, mind if I ask you a question?" "Why, no, ma'am," said the pilot. "What is it?" The little old lady said, "Did we land, or were we shot down?"

Courtroom Follies

Anonymous

The following were recorded on transcripts from actual courtrooms:

Q: What is your date of birth?
A: July fifteenth.
Q: What year?
A: Every year.

Q: What gear were you in at the moment of the impact?
A: Gucci sweats and Reeboks.

Q: All your responses must be oral, OK? What school did you go to?
A: Oral.

Q: How old is your son—the one living with you?
A: Thirty-eight or thirty-five, I can't remember which.
Q: How long has he lived with you?
A: Forty-five years.
Q: What was the first thing your husband said to you when he woke that morning?
A: He said, "Where am I, Cathy?"
Q: And why did that upset you?
A: My name is Susan.

Q: Sir, what is your IQ?
A: Well, I can see pretty well, I think.

Q: Did you blow your horn or anything?
A: After the accident?
Q: Before the accident.
A: Sure, I played horn for ten years. I even went to school for it.

Q: Do you know if your daughter has ever been involved in the voodoo occult?
A: We both do.
Q: Voodoo?
A: We do.
Q: You do?
A: Yes, voodoo.

Q: Now, Doctor, isn't it true that when a person dies in his sleep, he doesn't know about it until the next morning?

Q: The youngest son, the twenty-year-old, how old is he?

Q: Were you present when your picture was taken?

Q: Was it you or your younger brother who was killed in the war?

Q: Did he kill you?

Q: How far apart were the vehicles at the time of the collision?

Q: You were there until the time you left, is that true?

Q: How many times have you committed suicide?

Q: So the date of conception [of the baby] was August 8th?
A: Yes.
Q: And what were you doing at that time?

Q: She had three children, right?
A: Yes.
Q: How many were boys?
A: None.
Q: Were there any girls?

Q: You say the stairs went down to the basement?
A: Yes.
Q: And these stairs—do they go up also?

Q: Mr. Slatery, you went on a rather elaborate honeymoon, didn't you?
A: I went to Europe, sir.
Q: And you took your new wife?

Q: How was your first marriage terminated?
A: By death.
Q: And by whose death was it terminated?

Q: Can you describe the individual?
A: He was about medium height and had a beard.
Q: Was this a male or a female?

Q: Is your appearance here this morning pursuant to a deposition notice which I sent to your attorney?
A: No, this is how I dress when I go to work.

Q: Doctor, how many autopsies have you performed on dead people?
A: All my autopsies are performed on dead people.
Q: Do you recall the time you examined the body?
A: The autopsy started around 8:30 P.M.
Q: And Mr. Demmington was dead at the time?
A: No, he was sitting on the table wondering why I was doing an autopsy.

They Said It in the Church Bulletin

Anonymous

- Miss Charlene Mason sang "I Will Not Pass This Way Again," giving obvious pleasure to the congregation.
- Bertha Belch, a missionary from Africa, will be speaking tonight at Calvary Memorial Church in Racine. Come tonight and hear Bertha Belch all the way from Africa.
- Members of the outreach committee will make calls on people who are not afflicted with any church.
- Evening massage—6:00 P.M.
- The audience is asked to remain seated until the end of the recession.
- Low Self-Esteem Support Group will meet Thursday from 7:00 to 8:30 P.M. Please use the back door.
- FASTING CONFERENCE. The cost for attending the Fasting and Prayer conference includes meals.
- Our youth basketball team is back in action—Wednesday at 8:00 P.M. in the recreation hall. Come out and watch us kill Christ the King.
- Ladies, don't forget the rummage sale. It's a chance to get rid of those things not worth keeping around the house. Don't forget your husbands.
- The peacemaking meeting scheduled for today has been canceled due to a conflict.
- Barbara remains in the hospital and needs blood donors for more transfusions. She is also having trouble sleeping and requests tapes of Pastor Jack's sermons.

- A songfest was hell at the Methodist church Wednesday.
- Thursday night Potluck Supper. Prayer and medication to follow.
- The rosebud on the altar this morning is to announce the birth of David, the sin of Rev. and Mrs. Adams.
- Weight Watchers will meet at 7:00 P.M. at First Presbyterian Church. Please use large double door at the side entrance.
- Don't let worry kill you, let the church help.
- For those of you who have children and don't know it, we have a nursery downstairs.
- This being Easter Sunday, we will ask Mrs. Lewis to come forward and lay an egg on the altar.

Strictly Classified

Anonymous

The following entries come from classified ads in newspapers:

- Free Yorkshire Terrier. 8 years old. Hateful little dog.
- Free puppies: 1/2 Cocker Spaniel, 1/2 sneaky neighbor's dog.
- Found: Dirty white dog. Looks like a rat . . . been out awhile . . . better be reward.
- Snow blower for sale . . . only used on snowy days.
- Tickle Me Elmo, still in box, comes with its own 1988 Mustang, 5L, auto excellent condition $6800.
- Full-sized mattress. 20 Yr. warranty. Like new. Slight urine smell.
- Nordic Track $300, hardly used, call Chubby.
- Bill's Septic Cleaning . . . "We haul American-made products."
- Georgia peaches, California grown—89 cents lb.
- Nice parachute: Never opened—used once.
- Tired of working for only $9.75 per hour? We offer profit sharing and flexible hours. Starting pay: $7–$9 per hour.
- Exercise equipment: Queen size mattress and box springs—$175.
- Our sofa will seat the whole mob. 100% Italian leather.
- Joining nudist colony! Selling washer & dryer $300.
- Open house. Body shapers toning salon. Free coffee and donuts.
- For sale by owner: Complete set of Encyclopedia Britannica. 45 volumes. Excellent condition. $1,000 negotiable. No longer needed. Recently married; wife knows everything.

CHAPTER THREE

Born to Laugh:
Of Humor
and Kids

When I grow up, I want to be a little boy.
–Joseph Heller

*When I was a kid
my parents moved a lot,
but I always found them.*
–Rodney Dangerfield

Kids:
The Original Workout

Chonda Pierce

People go to a lot of trouble to work out. Some will ride a bike for thirty minutes, climb steps for fifteen minutes, and run for another twenty. These are the people who can burn off enough calories to offset a dozen donuts, a lemon-filled éclair, and *three* bites of Death by Chocolate (using a tablespoon). These are people with no life.

And it doesn't matter how terrible they look, either. When they walk out of the gym all sweaty, sticky, messy, and oftentimes smelly, people will actually stop them to say, "Oh, you look wonderful!"—just because they know they've been working out.

My girlfriend Angela and I got a good workout just the other day. She called me at 7:00 A.M. and asked, "Are you dressed?"

"Blue spandex with a fuchsia oversized sweatshirt," I answered.

"Oh, that color has always looked so good on you," she said.

"Thanks. How about you?"

"Well, I just bought one of those jogging outfits, the kind made from that slick parachute material."

"What color? Purple, I hope."

"Purple."

I squealed. "I bet you look *soooo* cute."

"So, you're ready?" I asked.

"Yeah, come on over."

My kids were already at school, so I hopped in my van and headed over to Angela's.

When I arrived, I found she had started without me. She was lugging a car seat about the size of a small recliner out the front door. "I've got this, if you want to help Brittany," she called with a grunt. Brittany is her six-year-old daughter. (Angela's purple outfit did look great, and I told her so.)

Brittany still had her "sleepy" hair, so I grabbed a brush and pushed and pulled the bristles through the tangles. Then I twisted a rubber band around bunches of hair to make pigtails. "Looks good," I announced. "Now go brush your teeth."

Just then her three-year-old brother, Austin, dashed past me in his stocking feet. Angela was close behind, wagging one shoe at him as she ran. I found the other shoe in the living room, picked it up, and fell in behind Angela, who was behind Austin, who was heading up the stairs. Angela took two steps at a time until she reached the very top, where she crawled the last few. I paced myself, feeling the stretch and strain of each hamstring. I caught up with her at the top, where we both collapsed to catch our breath.

"Did you see which way he went?" she asked.

I looked down the hall in both directions and shook my head. "You go that way, I'll go this way. If he makes a move for the steps, yell and I'll head him off."

"Good plan."

We headed off in separate directions, both crawling for stealth— and because neither of us was ready to stand up just yet. I felt my lower abdominal muscles tighten with every baby crawl I took. Angela caught up with Austin at the foot of his Winnie the Pooh bed. Together we wrestled his shoes on him. Once we tied the laces, I stood and massaged my upper arms. That was tough.

"Okay," Angela announced, brushing her hair out of her face and fixing it back into the purple tie that matched her warm-up suit. "Is everyone ready to get in the van?" Austin took off like a shot, and we gave chase again. Down the stairs we went, my calves screaming out with every step.

Angela did five laps around the kitchen island before I took the baton and did four more. Then Austin swerved into the living room, and Angela swooped him up—just like we had planned. "Gotcha!" she said.

"I'll get the door," I panted.

"Meet you at the van," she said to me, holding Austin around his chest, his two feet squirming in all directions. Angela was holding on tight, biting her lip, reaching back for a little extra something I'm sure she never knew she even possessed, her face turning a shade that came close to matching that of her suit.

She plopped Austin into his car seat, and together we tugged and pulled and cinched harnesses, braces, and straps. Brittany was so much easier—just pull and click the grown-up seat belt. But her backpack weighed almost as much as Austin. I carried it from her upstairs bedroom and passed it off to Angela, who lugged it down the back steps and rolled it into the van with a giant "Umph!"

We both stood there for a few moments, catching our breath and studying our handiwork. With the sleeve of my new shirt, I dabbed at the beads of perspiration on my forehead while Angela adjusted her hair. "Ready to roll?" she asked me.

"Ready," I said. "You drive."

The drive through the neighborhood wasn't too bad, a few turns here and there, a few stop signs. But once we entered the main highway, the story was different. Still, Angela handled the traffic like the seasoned mom she is. She worked the turn signal, pumped the brakes, and mashed the gas pedal. I noticed that whenever she gripped the wheel, like during a lane change, her knuckles would turn white. Then, at a stop sign or traffic light, they would flush back red as she loosened her grip.

We went to Brittany's school first. I hopped out, yanked open the van's side door, and unfastened Brittany, who skipped along the sidewalk and into the building. I squat-lifted her backpack and waddled in behind her.

When I got back to the van, Angela already had swapped seats with me. She was flexing both hands to rub away the tingles and bring back the circulation. "Your turn," she said to me with a smile.

I started out slow and easy, but then the right turn signal went out. "Got a burnout on the right!" I called over to Angela. She nodded and rolled down her window. I did the same. When we reached Austin's day care, which happened to be on the right, I stuck out my left arm and pointed back over the van. And—just in case whoever was behind me didn't understand what I was doing—I began to pump my arm up and down, like one of those lighted signs where the arrow seems to be moving across the side of a building. I looked over and saw Angela hanging out the passenger window, stabbing a finger into the air in the direction of Austin's school. I'm sure we appeared very effective to those behind us—fuchsia and purple arms flashing out from each side.

We made the turn safely and unbound Austin, taking turns carrying him to his classroom because he didn't want to walk. When we left the day care, Angela drove us to the mall. We walked past the fitness center, where a lot of people were dressed just like us. We found a place in the food court that sold chocolate donuts and coffee and snacked until the stores opened.

Later we went shopping for more workout clothes. I bought a chartreuse top with black piping and some spandex pants to match. (Angela said I looked like a frog, but I was also thinking about the burned-out turn signal in her van and how important it can be to be visible.) Angela bought this adorable bright-yellow fleece sweatshirt for 60 percent off. She looked like a canary, but it would help with the turning also. On our way out, we passed someone we recognized from church.

"Hello," our friend said. She was dressed in an Ann Taylor business suit and really could have tucked her shirttail in. (She looked a bit slouchy.)

"Hi," we both said, clutching our new purchases. My collar was still damp with sweat, and my muscles still ached from Brittany's backpack, so I walked with a slight hitch. Angela's hair had come out of the purple tie, and she was trying to push it out of her face.

Our friend looked at us, then glanced up at the fitness center sign behind us. As if she had it all figured out, she smiled and said, "You girls are looking just wonderful!" I wished I could have said the same about her. But it goes to show, you can get away with a lot of disasters if you wear a sweat suit.

Pearls of Wisdom

Assorted Kids

Never trust a dog to watch your food."

Patrick, age 10

"When your mom is mad at your dad, don't let her brush your hair."

Taylia, age 11

"A puppy always has bad breath—even after eating a Tic-Tac."

Andrew, age 9

"Never hold a dustbuster and a cat at the same time."

Kyoyo, age 11

"If you want a kitten, start out by asking for a horse."

Naomi, age 15

"Felt-tip markers are not good to use as lipstick."

Lauren, age 9

"When you get a bad grade in school, show it to your mom when she's on the phone."

Alyesha, age 13

"When you want something expensive, ask your grandparents."

Matthew, age 12

"Never smart off to a teacher whose eyes and ears are twitching."

Andrew, age 9

"Wear a hat when feeding seagulls."

Rocky, age 9

"Never flush the john when your dad's in the shower."

Lamar, age 10

"Forget the cake, go for the icing."

Cynthia, age 8

Masterpiece

Anonymous

A kindergarten teacher was observing her classroom of children as they drew. She would occasionally walk around to see each child's artwork.

As she got to one little girl who was working diligently, she asked what the drawing was.

The girl replied, "I'm drawing God."

The teacher paused and said, "But no one knows what God looks like."

Without missing a beat or looking up from her drawing, the girl replied, "They will in a minute."

God Is Watching

Anonymous

Up at the head table in the cafeteria, one of the nuns had placed a big bowl of bright-red, fresh, juicy apples. Beside the bowl she placed a note that read, "Take only one. Remember, God is watching."

At the other end of the table was a bowl full of freshly baked chocolate chip cookies, still warm from the oven. Beside the bowl there was a little note, scrawled in a child's handwriting, which read, "Take all you want. God's watching the apples."

Ultimate Sacrifice

Anonymous

One Sunday morning the pastor noticed little Alex staring up at the large plaque that hung in the church foyer. It was covered with names, and small American flags were mounted on both sides. The seven-year-old had been staring at the plaque for some time, so the pastor walked up, stood beside the boy, and said quietly, "Good morning, Alex."

"Good morning, Pastor," replied the young man, still focused on the plaque. "Pastor McGhee, what is this?" Alex asked.

"Well, son, it's a memorial to all the men and women who have died in the service." Soberly, Alex and the pastor stood together, staring at the large plaque.

Little Alex's voice was barely audible as he turned to the pastor and asked, "Which one—the 9:00 or the 10:30 service?"

Dear God

Assorted Kids

Dear God,

Maybe Cain and Abel would not kill each other so much if they had their own rooms. It works with my brother.

Larry

Dear God,

I read the Bible. What does "begat" mean? Nobody will tell me.

Love, Allison

Dear God,

Did you mean for the giraffe to look like that, or was it an accident?

Love, Norma

Dear God,

Who draws the lines around the countries?

Nan

Dear God,

Instead of letting people die and having to make new ones, why don't you just keep the ones you have?

Timmy

Dear God,

Thank you for the baby brother, but what I prayed for was a puppy.

Love, Joyce

Dear God,

If we come back as something, please don't let me be Jennifer Horton, because I hate her.

Denise

Dear God,

We read Thomas Edison made light. But in Sunday school they said you did it. So I bet he stole your idea.

Sincerely, Donna

Dear God,

I didn't think orange went with purple until I saw the sunset you made on Tuesday. That was cool.

Love, Sam

"Bet I Can!"

Marilyn Meberg

Sometimes I think about the "least likely" humans I have known, those who seemed incapable of letting a smile, giggle, or laugh escape from their frozen lips.

Eighty-year-old Mrs. Davidson falls into the frozen-lip category. Yet, as a child I found her fascinating. A good part of my fascination was undoubtedly that she would occasionally shout out disagreements during my father's preaching. I, on the other hand, wasn't even allowed to interrupt during second-grade reading group, much less during Dad's sermons. I was tremendously envious of all she got away with.

Since she lived within walking distance of our parsonage, I loved dropping in on her. She never seemed particularly glad to see me; instead she appeared indifferent to my visits.

One night at supper my parents quizzed me about why I liked visiting Mrs. Davidson. I think they were concerned that she might find me a nuisance or that she might hurt my feelings. I told my parents I liked her animals and loved the smell of her few bales of alfalfa, but more than that, I wanted to make her laugh. Both parents put down their forks and looked kindly at me.

"Honey," my father said, "I've never even seen Mrs. Davidson smile, much less laugh."

One of the things we did as a small family of three was make various bets. Dad always was betting my mother about some academic subject he was sure he was right about, only to find out he was totally wrong. That never seemed to squelch his enthusiasm, however, and the bets continued as long as they lived.

Thinking I might get in on the betting game, I said to my parents, "I'll bet I can get Mrs. Davidson to laugh before I'm in the third grade!" Rising to the challenge, they agreed and said they hoped I would win the bet. Mom asked what kind of payoff I wanted.

"French toast for breakfast every Saturday morning for six weeks," I said without hesitation.

For at least a month I tried every conceivable thing I could think of to make Mrs. Davidson laugh. I told her jokes; I told her all the bad things Lester Courtney did in school; I even did acrobatics for her. No response.

Then one day, as I was heading up the path toward her messy property, I was attempting to perfect my imitation of how Mr. Brownell walked. Mr. Brownell had caught his leg in a threshing machine at some point in his life, and the accident resulted in the most memorable walk I'd ever seen. Whenever his weight landed on his bad leg, his whole body would veer dangerously out of balance. But somehow the flapping of his arms caused him to catapult in the opposite direction until everything appeared to be back in order. His head moved in perfect rhythm to all this disjointedness. It was quite a feat.

I had been working on this imitation for some time—purely for my own sense of accomplishment. My efforts were interrupted by the sound of what could only be likened to a donkey's braying. It grew louder and louder until finally I located where the noise was coming from. Mrs. Davidson was leaning against the side of her chicken house—laughing. She laughed so long, so loud, and so hard it made me a little nervous. It seemed to me that making that much noise could kill a person.

"Well, Mr. Brownell," she finally gasped, "how nice of you to visit me," and then she went into another braying episode.

When I triumphantly announced to my parents that I had won the bet, they were concerned that the laughter had come at the expense of another's misfortune. I explained that I had been working on the walk for weeks but never intended it to be used for Mrs. Davidson. In fact, I further explained, I had no idea she was watching me until I heard her laugh. Apparently convinced that my heart was not cruel, I was rewarded with French toast every Saturday for six weeks.

"Yes, Ma'am!"

Sheila Walsh

My son, Christian, and I often revisit a familiar discussion on manners. He does well for a four-year-old boy, but he seems to have the Walsh trait of brain leakage, and occasionally all my reminders slip out.

We were flying to Dallas, Texas, and the flight attendant asked Christian if he would like to have wings to pin on his ball cap.

"Yes, I would!" he replied enthusiastically.

"Yes, ma'am," I reminded him.

"Yes, ma'am," he mimicked, looking at me as though I might be ruining his chances of having a meaningful relationship with this darling blond flight attendant.

Later that night he sat on my lap while we sang our favorite nighttime songs. When we were finished, I asked him if he remembered our discussion on the plane.

"Yes, ma'am," he replied with a grin.

"I know you think I make a fuss about things like that, Christian, but it's important to show respect for your elders."

He looked at me and laughed. He waited for me to join in. I didn't.

"Mommy, that was funny," he said, a little confused.

"Why was that funny?" I asked sternly.

"How can I show respect for my elbows?"

How often do we do that with the Lord? He says, "Trust"; we hear, "Try." He says, "Rest"; we hear, "Strive." He says, "I love you just the way you are"; we hear, "I love you, but I'd love you a bit more if you'd change a few of your bad habits."

Thank you, Father, that you're willing to keep talking to me, even when I don't get it! Amen.

Dig deep into the Word of God. All the right words are in there!

Kids Say the Craziest Things

Assorted Kids and Adults

I had been teaching my three-year-old daughter, Caitlin, the Lord's Prayer. For several evenings at bedtime, she would repeat after me the lines of the prayer. Finally, she decided to go solo. I listened with pride as she carefully enunciated each word, right up to the end of the prayer: "Lead us not into temptation," she prayed, "but deliver us some e-mail. Amen."

And one particular four-year-old prayed, "And forgive us our trash baskets as we forgive those who put trash in our baskets."

A little boy was overheard praying: "Lord, if you can't make me a better boy, don't worry about it. I'm having a real good time like I am."

A Sunday school teacher asked her little children, as they were on the way to the church service, "And why is it necessary to be quiet in church?" One bright little girl replied, "Because people are sleeping."

The preacher was wired for sound with a lapel mike, and as he preached, he moved briskly about the platform, jerking the mike cord as he went. Then he moved to one side, getting wound up in the cord and nearly tripping before jerking it again. After several circles and jerks, a little girl in the third pew leaned toward her mother and whispered, "If he gets loose, will he hurt us?"

A woman invited some people to dinner. At the table, she turned to her six-year-old daughter and said, "Would you like to say the blessing?" "I wouldn't know what to say," the girl replied. "Just say what you hear Mommy say," the wife answered. The daughter bowed her head and said, "Lord, why on earth did I invite all these people to dinner?"

My four-year-old son, Kyle, was unsuccessfully trying to open a bottle of children's vitamins. After watching several vain attempts, I explained, "It's made so only mommies and daddies can open it." After tiring of his struggle, Kyle relinquished the bottle. As I easily opened it for him, Kyle stared in amazement and asked in a breathless voice, "How does it know you're a mommy?"

Angela Mitchell, Kansas

My eight-year-old daughter, Candace, loves to spend time at her grandma's house. But I wondered if she spent too much time there when recently she sat down and started fanning herself, saying, "Whew! I'm having a hot flash. I hate hot flashes!"

Rebecca Stuhlmiller, Washington

When her dog and a pet goat died, my five-year-old stepniece, Whitney, was told that the animals were now in heaven. All was well for a few weeks—until Whitney and her mother, Ella, went for a walk. Ella explained that God made the flowers, the trees, and the bugs. "Where's God?" Whitney asked. "In heaven," her mother replied. Whitney moaned sympathetically. "What happened to him?"

Robin Martinez, New Mexico

I was at the beach with my four-year-old son, Pauly, when we discovered a dead seagull lying in the sand. "Mommy, what happened to him?" Pauly asked. "He died and went to heaven," I told him. Pauly thought for a moment, then said, "Did God throw him back down?"

Mary L. Shaw, Florida

My son, Zachary—age four—came screaming out of the bathroom to tell me he'd dropped his toothbrush in the toilet. So I fished it out and threw it in the garbage. Zachary stood there thinking for a moment and then ran to my bathroom and came out with my toothbrush. He held it up and said with a charming little smile, "We better throw this one out, too, 'cause it fell in the toilet a few days ago."

Jacqueline Bay, British Columbia

Birthday Countdown

Barbara Johnson

Andy was miffed when he didn't get the part he wanted in the Christmas pageant. He had hoped for the role of Joseph but got stuck being the innkeeper. So Andy decided to pull a fast one and get even with Joseph when he came with Mary, looking for a place to stay.

"Come right in, folks," innkeeper Andy told them. "I've got plenty of room."

Perplexed, Mary looked at the startled Joseph, who quickly rose to the occasion.

"Hey, this place is a real dump," he said, poking his head inside. "I'd rather go out and sleep in the stable."

Whatever happened to the wit and wisdom that served us so well as kids? Why can't we employ them when middle age baffles us? Experts say innate creativity begins to disappear at about the age of eleven because we stop using it. We become progressively less curious and spontaneous.

Youth is not a time of life but a state of mind. It boldly takes risks, seeks adventure, hopes for the best, and displays courage. You are as young as your faith is strong.

The actor Jimmy Stewart stayed young until the day he died at the age of eighty-nine. Although extraordinarily talented, he remained genuinely touched by the fact that he was a celebrity.

One time a stranger put his hand out and said, "Mr. Stewart, I don't guess it means much to you, but I want you to know I think you're wonderful." Taking the man's hand to shake it, Jimmy held on to it tightly, looked him in the eye, and said, "It means everything to me."

We live out the kingdom of God within us when we treasure each other like that and when we find ways to turn unfortunate things around. Laughter is one of those ways. Laughter stirs the blood, expands the chest, electrifies the nerves, and clears the cobwebs from the brain. If you laugh a lot, when you are older all your wrinkles will be in the right places!

If you live to be one hundred, your heart will beat 3,681,619,200 times, pumping 27,323,260 gallons of blood weighing over one hundred tons. (If you end up tired, you've earned it!) Think about making every heartbeat a happy one.

Actually, I think living to be one hundred would be great, but living to fifty twice would be so much better. The way to do it is to get one year younger each year after your fiftieth birthday. So on your fifty-first birthday you turn forty-nine, at sixty you are forty, and so on. I'm not saying lie about your age; actually grow younger every year!

The first rule for this (you'll start looking younger, too) is to scatter joy to everyone you meet. There is no more effective beauty secret. The second rule is to exercise regularly—and the best heart workout is reaching down and lifting someone else up. The third and last rule is to guard your enthusiasm—in fact, let every experience in life multiply it.

You can't turn back the clock, of course, but you can wind it up again. As a recycled teenager, insanity may be your best means of relaxation. The secret to growing younger is counting blessings, not birthdays. Don't grow up; grow down. You'll know you're getting the idea when you begin buying cereal for the toy, not for the fiber.

If you keep it up long enough, sooner or later you'll grow down from teenager to toddler. Uh-oh, there is one thing about being a two-year-old that could take all the fun out of getting younger. Beware the toddlers' creed: *If I want it, it's mine. If it looks like mine, it is mine. If I take it away from you, it's mine. If I had it a little while ago, it's mine. If I give it to you and change my mind, it's mine.* No wisdom there; this breaks every rule of growing down. Skip this stuff, then hop and jump to infancy—that blissful time when you have no more responsibility than to eat and sleep and bask in the love of your family. No one will blame you for an occasional wakeful night or fussy afternoon. Dependent on others, enjoy the minutes as they fall through the hours—on your way to eternity.

CHAPTER FOUR

For Wives and Moms Only

When you get to the end of your rope,
tie a knot and hang on.
—Franklin Delano Roosevelt

Out of all the things I've lost in life,
I think I miss my mind the most.
—Anonymous

You'll Never Have to Dust Again

Chonda Pierce

I don't know why I said yes to the fellow—maybe because never having to dust again sounded so . . . romantic!

"You mean, not even a little?" I asked him on the telephone.

"If you get this thing set up right," he answered, "use it frequently—like every day—then you can take all your old dust rags and throw them away. And then there are the health benefits for your children."

"For the children?"

"Yes, ma'am. Helps them to breathe easier."

"Really?" Anything to help my children breathe easier must be a good thing.

"Oh, yeah."

"Well, then," I said, "I guess we need to talk."

"How about tomorrow night?" he asked. "I'll have someone in your neighborhood who will be glad to demonstrate our machine for you."

That sounded perfect, and so the next night I warned David—before he had a chance to take off his work boots and walk around in his stained socks, or loosen his belt or something like that—that we had company coming.

Soon a man showed up at the front door, carrying a big black notebook under one arm and dragging R2-D2 at his side.

"Come right in," I said.

"My name's Chuck." He let go of the little robot to shake our hands. We led him into the living room, and he wheeled his contraption right along with him. "So you hate to dust?"

"It's no big deal, really," David said.

"Hate it with a passion," I interjected.

"Then you're going to love this." Chuck took a seat on our sofa and plopped the big notebook down on the coffee table in front of him. "Oh, would it be possible to get a drink of water?"

I left and returned with a glass of water to find Chuck and David bent over the robot, examining and punching buttons.

"It's a vacuum cleaner!" David said, looking up and smiling. "Chuck says this thing will pick up a bowling ball!"

"Why would you want to pick up a bowling ball?" I asked.

"If it can pick up a bowling ball," explained Chuck, "imagine what it can do with a speck of dust."

David whistled at that overwhelming notion.

"Here's your water," I said, handing over the glass. "Now tell me about the no-dusting part again."

Chuck took the glass and turned it upside down so that water and ice plopped right on the carpet in the middle of the living room floor. "Oops," he said, but he didn't seem too upset about his mess. "Good thing I've got the model 500 series A with me." He plugged his contraption into the wall, pulled out a coiled hose, telescoped out a silver wand, flipped on a toggle switch, and with a whine and a blare, the squatty little machine came to life. Chuck aimed the nozzle at the puddle on the carpet. The ice rattled as it got sucked up the silver wand, and in two seconds the spot was clean and nearly dry.

"Wow!" David said, as the whine of the machine died down.

"Kind of loud, isn't it?" I said.

"I'll bet you can pick up nuts and bolts with that thing," said David.

Chuck nodded.

"And wood chips!"

Chuck nodded again.

"And–"

"What about the dust?" I interrupted before we wound up back at the bowling ball. "And the easier breathing for the children?"

Chuck's face brightened. "Ah, yes, the dust and the breathing. Let me explain that, but first, let me show you some pictures." He turned the black notebook so David and I could see it easily and then began to flip through some laminated pages. He turned until he came to a big color photo of a space alien with giant, toothy chompers and long, hairy legs, and an antlike body with big, bulging eyeballs. I pulled back in disgust.

"Scary, isn't it?"

My hand was over my mouth, and I was afraid I wouldn't be able to speak, so I just nodded.

"Caught a big bass once with something that looked like that." David leaned in to get a good look at the picture.

"This," began Chuck, tapping the alien in his notebook, "is a dust mite. The picture's been blown up about a hundred times because the real mite is only the size of a dust speck." Chuck paused to allow us to soak in the dust-sized alien.

"Ma'am, how many children do you have?" he asked me.

I found my voice and eked out a weak, "Two."

Chuck dropped his head, rubbed the back of his neck, moved his hand up to his forehead, rubbed his eyes, and finally landed at his chin before saying in a most somber voice, "Then you need to hear this."

"Hear what?" David said.

"That these dust mites," he thumped the big, glossy photo on the table, "could be everywhere in this house. Even in the beds where your children sleep—heaven forbid."

"How can we get rid of them?" I asked.

"How can we zap 'em?" David slapped a fist into an open palm.

Chuck walked over to his machine and unfastened the hose. "Just leave this off, pour water into this opening until it's full, and press the start button." He pressed the button again, and the thing whirred to life for the second time that evening. For a couple of minutes, a thunderous roar filled the room. He finally punched it off. "If you do that on a regular basis, no more dust, no more dust mites. And your children can breathe easier and rest peacefully."

"Not while it's running." David massaged his eardrums.

"And how long should I let this thing run?" I asked.

"About an hour," he said.

"An hour!? And how often?"

"Every day."

"Just don't leave any bowling balls out, right?" David said, but Chuck ignored him.

"And how much does something like this cost?" David asked.

Chuck pointed at the picture of the dust mite on my coffee table and said, "To rid your home and your children's beds of these ... these ungodly creatures—sixteen hundred dollars."

David's eyes grew as large as the dust mite's enlarged one hundred times. "We didn't pay that much for our car."

Chuck broke all the numbers down for us. He even told us how many dust mites could fit on the head of a pin and explained that, with one push of a button, we could wipe out thousands, maybe even millions, of the little buggers. When it became clear to David how we actually were paying less than a penny per mite, the deal wasn't such a bad one after all.

And me? Well, I wheeled that little robot man all over the house and sucked up pillows and curtains and Legos and little green army men—and got real close to the cat once. For a while, I would turn on the machine every day and leave it in the middle of the room to roar and whine for at least an hour, sucking up the evil dust mites.

Twelve years later, we still have that old machine—and it's paid for now. I don't know how many dust mites were conquered with it over the years. Probably not many, because the thing was too stinking loud to live with. Sometimes David would hop about on the carpet and then announce to me that he had squashed enough for today, just so I wouldn't turn on the machine. Other times he and the children would hop around and have big dust mite–squashing parties. I would always make refreshments.

Sometimes our good intentions can drown out what's really important to a family. David and I wanted so badly to wage war against all the dust mites of the world. But what God reminded me of—and in the roar of a vacuum cleaner, no less—was that there are more important things we can do for our children, such as teach them the truths of God. And that's hard to do with something as loud as a 747 roaring in the living room every day.

Our battle against dust mites goes on. Today, when we sit down on a sofa for family time, we like to think we squashed a few for the cause. But what we have to pass on to our children doesn't have anything to do with a vacuum cleaner.

So if you're interested in a vacuum that can pick up bowling balls, it'll be at our next yard sale—financing available.

What Part of "Ten Items or Less" Don't You Understand?

Chonda Pierce

The young woman's hand seemed to move in slow motion. All I could do was stand—frozen—and watch as she reached higher and higher, until her fingers twisted around a cotton string that was attached to a beaded chain that was attached to a light switch. With a quick yank on the string, the plastic number three began to blink. Then, still in slow motion, she lifted a black phone from its cradle and spoke into its mouthpiece. Her tired voice rang throughout the store: "Price check on aisle three, please. Price check on aisle three." It looked like another long day at Stal-Mart.

And I was next in line, too! I thought I had picked a good line. The woman in front of me had only two items—but one of those turned out to be a turtleneck sweater with no price tag. After the cashier made her announcement, she stepped away from the register, folded her arms, and leaned against the wall of her little cubicle, getting comfortable. Now, this was not the first price check I'd lived through—housewares, electronics, kids' wear, I'd had lots of experience. But women's wear was big trouble.

I know women who will pick up a blouse and fall in love with it. But as the day goes on, usually somewhere in the automotive section, the love affair ends, and the blouse is left hanging from a spark-plug display. "It's okay," the woman says. "It gives the workers something to do." And I'm convinced that part of the workers' job is to remove the price tag before they find its real home.

By the time that blouse can be matched up with similar blouses that do have a price tag, I was thinking, *my ice cream will be melted, my cab-*

bage wilted. Yes, I should have known that a turtleneck sweater was trouble.

I gritted my teeth, gripped the buggy handle, and pulled back from aisle three. For a moment I just hovered in the No-Buy Zone—you know, that big area in front of the registers where you don't shop, but you cruise back and forth in search of the perfect checkout line. I noticed the light for aisle seven was on, so I set out. My wheels squawking, I yanked the cart a hard right rather than try to roll the long way around the popcorn display. (Someone always puts up the oddest displays in the No-Buy Zone. Cheaper than speed bumps, I guess.)

Aisle seven would take you even if your cart was crammed full and overflowing—or even pulling a second cart in tow, like the train that cut me off. The train's driver saw me coming, I know she did, and if it hadn't been for the box of Cap'n Crunch that came flying out of the second cart, I'd have beat her to the belt. But I had to brake hard to avoid the cereal box, which allowed her carts to zip in just before mine. The mother ushered and tugged her buggies into the channel. With a hard look, I studied the toddler in the second cart as it passed by me. He was grinning, mouth smeared with something sweet. He waved at me and pointed at the Cap'n Crunch. I smelled a conspiracy.

No time to lament. I spun the cart 360 degrees (barely missing the display for Titanic bath soap).

Number three was still flashing, the cashier still resting. But now light one was on—and the lane was empty! I pushed the cart hard and felt my cargo shift. On the way past three, I noticed the woman who wanted the turtleneck was pulling and tugging at the sweater, searching inside the neck, under the arms, everywhere, for that elusive price tag.

I slowed and cruised into aisle one at a safe speed. There to greet me was a young girl with lavender eye shadow, green lipstick, and black fingernail polish. (I am not making this up.) In between the chomping sounds she made on her wad of bubble gum (bigger than my fist), she was talking to the cashier at the register next to her about Billy Earl and something about a fistfight with Ernestine and how "Mama's done kilt 'em both." (I'll interpret for you later.) In the middle of her sentence, she glanced my way for a split second, long enough to say, "Sorry, ma'am, but this is the express lane. Five items or less." I kept waiting for her to say, "Just kidding" or, "Come on in. I'll take you anyway," but she didn't.

Rather than move, I studied my load. I didn't have too much. "I think I'm close on the count here," I told her, ashamed at how pleading my voice sounded.

Just about the time Billy Earl had done went down to Tucson and bought a double-wide, she put one hand on her hip and finally looked at me. "Maybe you are close," she said. "But sometimes we have customers who have small emergencies, like sick children at home, or they've run out of diapers, or they need batteries for their flashlights because the power has been knocked out. Things like that. That's what this aisle here is for, so people with real emergencies don't have to wait so long."

I looked back. There was no one behind me. "There are no emergencies right now!"

She chose not to hear this and instead said, "Perhaps you should try …" she paused as she scanned across the aisles, "… aisle three. It looks like she can take you over there." And she went back to planning her outfit for whenever Billy Earl got back from Tucson.

I looked over to aisle three and saw that the light was on and not flashing. "You're serious?" I asked. I studied the hostess of aisle one, but all she did was shrug her pretty little shoulders and say, "Store policy."

I jerked the buggy backwards, the wheels grinding and bouncing and leaving a dotted black skid mark on the tile floor that someone would later probably have to use a giant buffer to remove.

The cashier at aisle three saw me coming; I know she did. And I saw her leaning back against her little cubicle, arms folded, yawning. I clipped a tin of popcorn on the way past and sent it wobbling into the path of an oncoming buggy. I thought about the little toddler in buggy number two, tossing out boxes of Cap'n Crunch that worked like mortar shells to keep incoming buggies away, and felt rather proud of this tactic. But before I arrived at the conveyor belt, before I could grab up that little baton and slap it down on the black surface to keep someone else's groceries from getting mixed up with mine, the yawning cashier picked up a cone-shaped object that advertised cigarettes and set it down on the belt. Below the advertisement was the note, "This Register Closed."

"You mean *after* me, right?" I said.

"Sorry, but it's my break time." She yawned, slipped out of her cubicle, and walked away.

"Aisle seventeen is open with no waiting," blared a voice over the PA system. Again I reversed out of the aisle and turned my buggy in the direction of aisle seventeen, which was so far away I doubted my own strength and stamina to make it that far, just past the flea and tick display. Frozen in place, I couldn't move. In moments, my heart slowly sank as I watched a tiny buggy (at least it looked tiny from that far away) slip into the spot marked aisle seventeen. I could only lean forward on my buggy, parked motionless beside a cardboard cutout of the Titanic, and watch my hope slip away. But I wasn't going to cry.

I knew then that I had no other option. I began to throw items overboard—Pringles, plastic coat hangers, shoe polish, some fuzzy socks with rubber grips on the bottoms, and at least a half-dozen other odds and ends—until I was down to five items. (The socks dangled dangerously from the bow of the Titanic, but that would give the workers something to do.) Then, with renewed determination, I turned my buggy about and aimed again for aisle number one—the express lane.

"Hi, remember me? Just waiting to hear if Billy Earl got the double-wide back to Tennessee." (Okay, I'll admit I said it with a bit of sarcasm. She was not amused.) Before she could say anything, I told her, "I have five items, and I'm in a hurry—this is an *emergency.*"

She smiled because that was what she was supposed to do. "Did you find everything you needed today?" she asked, as she began to scan my items.

I had kept a pair of big, fuzzy house shoes, and she picked them up and studied them as though they were a puppy. "How cute!" she squealed. She turned them over once, twice, without finding what she was looking for. When she reached for the cotton string that dangled just above her head—the string that was attached to the chain that was attached to the flashing light—I grabbed the shoes from her and laid them on the chewing-gum rack beside the register.

"I'll get those some other time," I said.

She looked confused. "But they're *so* cute!"

I took my four items and left, wadding up my shopping list and stuffing it into my pocket as I walked. Before I could get to the door, I heard a voice on the PA. I recognized it as the sleepy voice of the cashier on aisle three. She was asking for a price check from women's wear on a pair of fuzzy socks with rubber grips on the bottoms.

Later that evening, my husband called to tell me he was on his way home. "Can I pick up anything for you on my way?"

I pulled the crumpled shopping list out of my pocket and flattened it out on the counter. "As a matter of fact," I said, "while you're out . . ."

Gourmet Napping

Becky Freeman

I used to think I didn't have time for such luxuries. A nap? Are you kidding? In the middle of my hectic day? Puh-lease. Or I might take one but wake up feeling frazzled and guilty. There was always this fast-forward tape going on in my head, taunting me with a singsong, "You're getting behind-er, you're getting behind-er." I thought if I just kept doing and doing, staying focused on my to-do list, no matter what—or who—interrupted my day, I could actually, eventually, catch up.

Then one bright morning, I had this incredible moment of enlightenment and realized The Truth. There is no such place as "All Caught Up." It only exists out there in our imaginations along with Oz and Santa's Workshop and Never-Never Land.

Why didn't the grown-ups tell us this when we were kids? I don't know, I simply don't know. Perhaps they, too, are still struggling under the illusion that it exists somewhere out there. You may have to grieve a little over the loss of this fairy-tale catch-up land. You'll find it a healthy, cleansing experience, though. Because in the long run, I guarantee you'll be thankful I told you the hard truth right now—before you waste any more time chasing a dream. When you give up on the existence of "All Caught Up," you are free to do all those wonderful things you were waiting to do until you arrived there. Like, for example, taking a guilt-free nap.

I have learned, the hard way, that taking a short nap is the best thing I can do when I'm plagued with hurry-upitis. I used to cram, pray, recite, and practice before a speech. Now I look for a good place to snooze for twenty minutes instead. I'm convinced that God goes inside our brains and cleans house in there when we resign control of the universe long enough to let go and drift into a short sleep.

I've actually elevated napping to a gourmet experience. Let's say it's a springtime afternoon loaded with deadlines, housework, phone calls, and a hundred obligations, and I begin to feel the pressure building inside. (I love the title of Julie Barnhill's new book *She's Gonna Blow!* Any woman who's been there knows what built-up tension feels like and how everyone around you can pick it up.)

Like a movie producer who yells, "Cut!" I've learned to stop, walk away from the middle of the action, and melt like a boneless chicken into my quilt-laden hammock.

I soak up the warmth of sunshine on my skin and watch the play of light on the leaves in the trees overhead. Then I imagine my brain is a lot like the world before God fixed it up: dark, formless, and void. Very void. And I pray, "Father, hover over me the way you hovered over the formless deep, and create order out of the chaos that is now my mind."

As I imagine myself cocooned in his Spirit, I almost always fall into a deep, peaceful sleep. Then I wake up in a few minutes, refreshed, without a trace of guilt.

CAN YOU BELIEVE IT? Trust me, this sort of experience has been a long time in coming. Now there are books on Power Napping, and a number of corporations are even beginning to create Napping Rooms—realizing that the long-lasting effects of fifteen minutes of rest are more effective than caffeine infusions from the coffee station.

"How can I stop for a nap when I have so much I should be doing?" you may ask. Here is the answer. You get three times as much accomplished in one well-rested hour as you do in three hours of plodding along half awake. Take an hour to sleep and an hour to work, and you gain a whole extra hour to play with. Okay, I'll admit I just made that up. But you're just going to have to trust me on this one.

For you more scientific types, I do have some objective research proving that one nap a day will increase the number of your highly creative periods. It has to do with hypnopomping and hypnagogging. Really. I'm not making this up.

Hypnopomping actually refers to that period of time just before we are completely awake, when our mental pictures are a mixture of dreams and our own created images. It is considered one of the most productively creative periods. Hypnagogging, on the other hand, is that time just before we are asleep. Again, it is when images are a mixture of dreams and thoughts under our control—another highly creative state of mind.

Thomas Edison had an unusual technique for putting that hypnagogic state to work. He would doze off in a chair with his arms and hands draped over the armrest. In each hand he held a ball bearing, and below each hand on the floor were two pie plates. When he drifted into the state between waking and sleeping, his hands would naturally relax and the ball bearings would drop on the plates. Awakened by the noise, Edison would immediately make notes on any ideas that had come to him.

I wish someone would explain why, if we are such a brilliantly advanced nation, American forefathers let the concept of a Nationwide Nap slip through the cracks of the Constitution? I appreciate that Ronald Reagan took naps while he was president. I, for one, miss having him in the Oval Office—relaxed enough to take a little snooze now and then. His mere napping presence was soothing. (After all, if *the president* could nod off, what was there for the rest of us to worry about?)

In Latin America, they deal with midafternoon slumps by embracing The Siesta. The English have a countrywide sleepy-time breather they disguise as a tea party. Again, it takes place in the late afternoon, and because the English are the way they are, they call it High Tea. One of England's most celebrated citizens, William Shakespeare, penned the poignant words, "O, sleep, O gentle sleep [beloved nap time!], Nature's soft nurse."

Indeed, a short sleep is a healing balm.

Now, if you'll excuse me, the birds are tweeting outside my office window, the quilt-covered hammock is calling—and so off to hypnagog I go.

Chatting with Martha Stewart about My *To-Do* List

Chonda Pierce

Last night I had another dream about Martha Stewart. She showed up at my house early in the morning, just after the kids had gone to school. We sat in my huge sunroom (which I don't have in real life—that's how I knew it was a dream) and talked like old girlfriends while a small jazz ensemble played in a far corner by the fountain that had real koi fish swimming about and several thousand dollars in change underwater where people had stopped to make a wish. Martha and I were sipping our coffee. (Just some cheap decaffeinated stuff I had bought at Kroger's.)

"So your kids are in school?" she asked.

"Oh, yes. Long ago," I answer.

"Children are so cute," she said, sipping her coffee. "I would love to have watched them make their own breakfasts and prepare their own lunches to take."

"Me, too."

"You mean you didn't watch them?"

"I mean they didn't make their own breakfasts, let alone their own lunches."

She set down her coffee cup slowly and said, "You mean you prepared for both of them?"

"*And* myself *and* my husband."

"Oh, my." Her forehead wrinkled.

"Oh, Martha, enough about that. I've been dying to ask you something. On that show you did last Christmas, did you really make your own salt and pepper?"

Martha cut a glance about the room to make sure we were alone (with the exception of the jazz ensemble and the fish, of course). Then she confided, "I have to be honest."

I leaned in closer.

"Someone else quarried the salt."

"No!"

She nodded. "Of course, I grew and harvested the pepper and ground it myself. *And* I filled the shakers." She smiled and seemed pleased with herself. She nodded her approval to the jazz ensemble and then looked around the room. "This is such a lovely room. Did you make it?"

"Oh, heavens no. Are you kidding? I just dreamed this thing up. I have so much laundry to do, when would I find time to make glass and glue it together like you would?"

"Laundry? What do you mean by laundry?"

"You know, separating the darks from the whites, the towels from the delicates."

"Then what?"

"Then I put them in the washer, add soap—"

"I can make soap."

"Make sure all the socks are turned right-side-out—"

"All of them?"

I nodded. "And then dry—"

"Dry?"

"And fold—"

"Fold?"

"And put away."

"Where?"

"Why, into the proper chest of drawers or closet. Or at least in neat little stacks in the corner of the room."

"I hadn't thought about that. So how long does a job like that last?" she wanted to know.

I paused for a long moment—for effect, I admit, and to give her an opportunity to swallow her last drink of coffee—before saying deliberately, *"Forever."*

She put a hand to her mouth, and I feared maybe I hadn't paused long enough. "I hadn't thought about that," she said.

"Oh, please," I said, "enough about laundry. Do tell me about that crumpet party I saw on your show once."

"Crumpets are boring," she said.

"Then tell me about how you made your own paper for the invitations."

She dismissed this with a wave and said, "Just like any other paper—wood pulp, et cetera." Then, lowering her cup from a fresh swallow, she asked, "Have you ever vacuumed your carpet?"

I nodded.

"I mean, like a *whole* room?"

"Try a whole house," I said, trying not to sound as though I were bragging.

She gasped.

"And then I usually dust," I added.

"Dust what?"

"The furniture."

"I can build furniture," she said.

"I know, Martha, and you're quite good."

Just then the phone rang, and I answered, "Oh, yes, I'm expecting you. I'll be here with Martha Stewart . . . Okay, I'll ask." I covered the phone and asked Martha, "The plumber wants to know why the hot water valve is always on the left and cold on the right."

"Tell him," Martha said, "to watch this Sunday's program."

"Watch her this Sunday," I said into the phone. "Besides, this is *my* dream, and I'm having my *own* chat." I hung up and said, "That was the plumber. He'll be here in a bit."

"Plumber? For what?"

"Toilet's stopped up."

She set down her coffee and pushed it away. "How do you do it?"

"Do what?"

"Take care of your children and your husband, do the laundry, vacuum, dust the furniture, take out the trash—you do take out your own trash?"

"Only when it's full."

"And *then* cook?"

I nodded, but I had never thought of my day as quite so overwhelming, so daunting a task, until I heard Martha Stewart lay it out so plainly.

I shrugged and said, "Practice, I guess."

The plumber showed up, gave Martha a big hug, and told her how great her spinach quiche recipe was. He dragged out a big coiled cable with a giant electric motor that uncoiled the cable across the room and into my toilet. After a few moments, the plumber spun it backwards and pulled out Bongo, my son's favorite Beanie Baby.

"So *that's* where that went!" I said, spraying it down with some Shout and dropping it into the washer, which was set for the very next load. Zach would be excited when he got back from school.

The plumber asked for Martha's autograph (on an old nasty plunger of all things), picked up his auger, and left.

I retrieved a mop from the garage and wiped up some size-thirteen prints from the vinyl floor.

"*Why* do you do this?" Martha asked, the exasperation evident in her voice.

"Do what?"

"All this," and she waved an arm about my big sunroom, but she meant my whole house. "The laundry, the dusting, the vacuuming, the mopping—"

"Don't forget the windows."

"You do windows? *Why?* Couldn't you just hire someone to take care of menial tasks like these so you would have more time for other things, like weaving napkins with an interlaced monogram or crafting reproductions of Early American Shaker furniture?"

Now that the plumbing seemed to be taken care of, I filled Martha's cup with more coffee. The dark liquid warmed the cup; sunshine poured through the glass overhead and warmed everything else. I noticed the streaks and the dust, so I added "Clean the sunroom" to my to-do list. I'd take care of it as soon as Martha left.

I carried the pot of coffee back to the kitchen and dragged the mop behind me, thinking about Martha's question. The jazz ensemble was playing something perky now as I answered her. "Perhaps in *your* dreams things like that can happen, Martha, but not in mine."

Glancing at my watch, my heart thumped. Any minute my kids would be barreling in the door looking for an after-school snack. I pulled a box of Little Debbie snack cakes out of the cupboard and laid them on a plastic plate. No, I didn't make them myself, but the kids won't care. They'll be too busy ripping open the wrappers, and I'll be too busy hearing about their day. I'm pretty comfortable with that. Suddenly I felt a little sad for Martha.

On the way past the fountain, I flipped in a quarter and made a wish.

CHAPTER FIVE

Lookin' So Good!

The LORD seeth not as man seeth;
for man looketh on the outward appearance,
but the LORD looketh on the heart.
–The Bible, 1 Samuel 16:7 KING JAMES VERSION

My idea of strenuous exercise
is to fill the bathtub and lie back,
then pull the plug and fight the current.
–Barbara Johnson

The Bra of My Dreams

Cathy Lee Phillips

The Madras School girl's rest room was packed with fourth graders washing up after morning recess. I was elbowing my way through the crowd when Betsy Fowler's shrill voice rang out above the chatter.

"Well, look at this. My bra strap just won't stay in place."

An uneasy silence enveloped the Madras School girl's rest room. Betsy shoved a very obvious white strap underneath the shoulder of her sleeveless pink and white polka-dot shirtwaist dress and smiled smugly.

I hated her at that moment.

It didn't matter that, being the largest girl in the class, she would naturally be the first to need a bra. It didn't matter that, as an only child, Betsy was constantly showered with gifts from adoring parents. All that mattered was that Betsy Fowler was the first girl in the Madras School fourth grade to wear a bra, and she had succeeded in making the rest of us aware of the fact. Though it was not discussed openly, I firmly believe that, right then, every girl in that rest room silently vowed to secure a bra before sundown. Me included.

Needless to say, I concentrated little on science and arithmetic the rest of that Monday afternoon. I wanted a bra in the worst way, and by the time the final bell rang it was an obsession. I rode the bus home in silence, daydreaming of the scene that would surely unfold when I arrived home. I would walk up to Mama and calmly announce, "Mother, it is time. I must have a bra."

She would take me in her arms and shower me with kisses while shedding a bucket of maternal tears over how quickly I had grown up. Together we would drive to town, where, with great ceremony, we would choose the perfect bra. It would be pure white, decorated with lace and a tiny pink flower adorning the front. In my fantasy, this would be a special day my mother and I would recall fondly for the rest of our lives.

As the bus stopped, I jumped off and raced up the driveway. Mama stood at the kitchen sink, and—my fantasy abruptly abandoned—I blurted, "Betsy Fowler has a bra, and I've just got to get one!"

Mama slowly dried her hands. She took one step back and looked at me squarely for several agonizing seconds before muttering five horrible little words: "You don't need a bra!"

Need? Who said anything about need? It never dawned on me that I *needed* a bra. The situation was simple: Betsy Fowler had a bra, and therefore I wanted one.

I didn't care about the job a bra performed. I was not suffering from "cleavage envy," nor did I want anything to put into the bra. I simply wanted a bra. Immediately! I wanted to stand in the Madras School girl's rest room and push a lacy white bra strap underneath the shoulder of a sleeveless dress.

The look on Mama's face, though, told me that she simply did not understand my situation. Furthermore, she had no intention of showering me with kisses, shedding maternal tears, or driving me to town for a precious white bra decorated with lace and a pink flower.

My fantasy died right there in the kitchen on Posey Road.

Life was brutal. By suppertime I was convinced that the next morning I would be the only fourth-grade girl attending Madras School braless. Horrified, I did what any other normal fourth-grade child would do—I nagged, I pestered, I whined. I accused my mother of not loving me, of not caring about either my reputation or my general well-being. I compared her unfavorably to mothers of my classmates. I brooded and sulked, while murmuring Betsy Fowler's name under my breath. I was obnoxious and bratty. But I was persistent, and when I climbed into bed on Thursday night, my godly and beleaguered mother surrendered.

"I will pick you up after school tomorrow, and we will go to town and buy you a trainer."

A TRAINER!?

I began to worry. A trainer? What was a trainer? Was it a bra? If so, was it lacy and white? Did it have a pink flower on the front? And furthermore, was I ready for a trainer? I didn't know training was involved in this particular growth process. Didn't the contents of a bra just grow naturally? What was I supposed to train them to do? And what if I trained them wrong? After all, I was only nine years old; without realizing it, I could disfigure myself for life. Training? This was a lot of responsibility to place on a fourth grader.

I hardly slept at all.

True to her word, Mama was waiting for me when the final school bell rang. My stomach hurt, and I was afraid I would throw up long before we walked into Kessler's on the Court Square in Newnan.

Inside, we met a tall lady with gray hair and tiny glasses perched on the end of her nose.

"We've come to purchase a bra," Mama announced. Over the top of her glasses the gray-haired lady looked at me with the same expression my mother had given me earlier in the week. She didn't say those five little words, but I knew she was thinking them.

"I think we need a trainer," she said. My stomach began to hurt again.

Taking a second look at me, she walked toward a rack holding small pastel boxes. She opened a blue box and held up a trainer. My stomach relaxed, and I began breathing normally. It was a bra—and it was perfect! It was a brilliant white. Lace decorated the bottom, and to my delight, a petite pink flower sat front and center. Trainer or not, it was the bra of my dreams. Surely Betsy Fowler had no finer bra.

"We'll take it," Mama announced. I left the store without saying a word, but as I walked toward the door, I was sure everyone was staring at me, fully aware that a bra rested inside my brown shopping bag.

Later, I placed the bra safely inside my top drawer, where it would remain until I dressed for school Monday morning. I slept peacefully that Friday night, quite happy with myself for getting exactly what I wanted.

Monday morning came. I awoke before the alarm sounded. My dress had been carefully chosen—pale yellow tulips on a blue background. It was sleeveless, of course, thus allowing my bra strap to make an appearance at a strategic moment during the school day. The garment felt quite strange, but I was confident it would feel more natural the longer I wore it. Climbing aboard the school bus, I felt like a true woman of the world. With one meager appearance of a simple bra strap, I planned to personally wipe that smug look off the face of Miss Betsy Fowler.

Arithmetic—definitely not my favorite subject—was my first class that day. To my surprise, I knew the answer to the first question the teacher asked. Raising my hand enthusiastically, I discovered, to my horror, that my bra went with it!

Instead of staying in its intended location, the garment slithered up my chest and crept rapidly toward my neck. I instantly lowered my hand and turned crimson with embarrassment. Were bras supposed to do this? Hoping no one was watching, I hunched over my desk, discreetly tugging and yanking, trying desperately to return the bra to its proper position.

As I made my final adjustments, the teacher called my name.

"Cathy, could you come to the board and show us how to work this problem."

I walked slowly to the front of the room, selected a piece of chalk, and lifted my arm to write the numbers on the blackboard. As I did, the bra lurched upward. It climbed toward my throat, twisting and pinching as it moved. Had some demon, intent on ruining my life, gained control of this innocent garment? The bra kept crawling higher and higher until it seemed ready to shoot through the neck of my dress. I was sure everyone in the class could see an abnormal wrinkle crisscrossing my chest. Holding me in its tight grip, the wicked combination of elastic and lace threatened my dignity and bound my upper chest until I could barely breathe.

Excusing myself quickly, I ran to the bathroom. I was no longer interested in showing my strap to Betsy Fowler and the other girls in my fourth-grade class. I was interested in pure, basic survival.

My mind raced as I jerked the bra back into place. What could I do with this cursed object? I had no purse. I couldn't just stuff it into one of my books. Surely one of the boys in class would find it, and I would die from the resulting ridicule. I couldn't throw the bra away—Mama would never let me hear the end of it. I couldn't call home sick and listen to my mama's "I told you so" the rest of the day.

There was no alternative. I had to wear the horrible contraption until the end of the day. I could do it, I told myself, as long as I didn't move my arms. Thus I spent the rest of the day walking like a short robot programmed to keep my arms glued tightly to my side.

I stepped off the bus that afternoon completely humiliated. Walking silently to my room, I removed that cursed garment and stuffed it in the back corner of my dresser drawer. I prayed I would never see it again.

Mama never mentioned the bra again. Neither did I. But when the time was right and I *needed* one, we returned to Kessler's and bought a suitable bra for me. Because I then possessed the necessary anatomical components, the bra stayed easily in place.

I have worn many bras since that horrible day at Madras School so long ago. I have worn underwires and cross-your-hearts. I have worn two-hookers, four-hookers, back-hookers, and front-hookers. I have worn T-backs, U-backs, posture bras, and sports bras. I have worn strapless bras, bras with comfort straps, and bras with frayed straps held together with a few strategically placed safety pins. I've worn white bras, black bras, ivory bras, and once, on a dare, a leopard-skin bra. Occasionally, I still wear a bra with a tiny pink flower on the front.

Ironically, there are now many times I don't *want* to wear a bra at all, but nowadays I really *need* one.

I can still recall clearly that awful day in the fourth grade. Would I have been more patient had I known just how many bras were in my future? Probably not. I was controlled completely by my wants. My needs were not an issue. And though quite a few years have passed since I was in the fourth grade, I still struggle with this same problem.

It is a hard thing to realize that I do not always know what is best for me. Mama knew best in the fourth grade. God knows best today and every day.

Grant me the wisdom I need, O Lord, to praise you for meeting my needs—and to trust your wisdom when it comes to controlling my wants.

Step Right Up

Patsy Clairmont

I can identify with Zacchaeus in that I have a difficult time finding a place high enough to let me see a parade. Visibility is limited when you're five feet tall. I've spent a lifetime on my tiptoes, calling up to others, "What's going on?"

I know I'm supposed to take comfort in the saying "dynamite comes in small packages." But I don't want to blow up; I want to grow up.

Sitting tall is also a challenge because invariably, a seven-foot-two-inch fellow will plant himself in front of me at church. I then have the joy of staring for the next hour at the seams in his shirt and his nappy neck. It's like trying to watch a ball game through a billboard.

Hugging is often a strain as we shorties have to reach past our stretching points to squeeze a neck. It's such a rumpling experience and requires readjusting everything from hat to hose.

As a speaker, I frequently find myself peeking over lecterns in my attempts to spot the audience. It's difficult to retain the interest of people when their view consists of your forehead and eyebrows. I have stood on many creative booster stools so I could see and be seen.

At one retreat, the kitchen workers brought me a box of canned juice to stand on. It worked fine until my high heel poked between two cans and I jerked sharply backward. I grabbed the lectern, catching myself just before doing a topsy-turvy somersault. My disheveled appearance resulting from my stage aerobics made me look juiced.

I have perched on many piano benches to speak. Because they're pieces of furniture, I always remove my shoes before stepping up. Smooth nylons on shiny-finished wood equals slick chick in action. It's like trying to speak on ice skates—possible but risky.

To elevate me enough to be seen at one church meeting, the staff quickly piled up two stacks of hymnals, five deep. As I turned to look at my audience from one side of the auditorium to the other, the books would swivel. At one point the right-foot stack headed east while the left-foot stack headed west. Those shifting stilts kept me divided in my concentration, as I was concerned I would leave with a split personality.

I've stood on milk crates, suitcases, tables, and kiddie stools. Once I was precariously placed on a wooden box whose weight limit I obviously exceeded. It creaked threateningly throughout my presentation as I closed in prayer, a soloist began to sing, and I cautiously stepped down. Relieved that I hadn't burst the boards, I walked down the platform steps to take a seat. At the last step, my heel caught in the microphone cords, and I crash-landed in the front row as the singer was belting out "Amazing Grace." I obviously was not Grace, although in a discussion later, we thought it was amazing I could survive my teeter-totter platform and then splat when I arrived on solid ground.

It's difficult to be taken seriously when you're sixty inches short. People have a habit of referring to shorties as "cute." "Cute" is what you call a toddler, a house without a future, or the runt of the litter.

I tried to increase the presentation of my stature by wearing tall clothes. But more than once, while walking up the front steps in sanctuaries, my heel slid into the hem of my long skirt, toppling me across the altar, where I looked like some sort of short sacrifice.

I shortened my skirts and added shoulder pads to my jackets in an effort to give an illusion of tallness without tripping myself.

Then one time I was in Washington, and when I was introduced, I grabbed my suit jacket and slid into it as I headed for the stage. I had been speaking for about fifteen minutes when I turned my head to one side and noticed that my left shoulder was four inches higher than my right. Evidently the pad, rather than conforming to the shape of my shoulder, perched on it. Up to that point, I was the only one in the auditorium who hadn't noticed. I was speaking on being dysfunctional and suggested that this perched pad was proof of my expertise in the subject. When I finished speaking, the mistress of ceremonies approached the steps with the back of her dress tucked into her panty hose. That took a lot of pressure off me.

Another time, I was sharing the stage with a statuesque and elegant friend who, as I was speaking, noticed that my mega shoulder pad had slid off my shoulder and into my blouse. She reached in through my neckline and fished down my back in her attempt to retrieve it. I was stunned but continued to speak as though I didn't notice she was shoulder-deep into my clothing. Well, I lost the audience as everyone became hysterical watching her catch my illusive inches and pat them securely back into place.

I wish my height were my only struggle with smallness. Unfortunately, I'm also shortsighted in my faith. I'm one of those "if I can see it, then I can believe it" people.

Zacchaeus was a small man who shinnied up a sycamore tree to give himself a boost. To that extent, I can identify. But his next move made the difference for him in a way lengthened robes or mountainous shoulder pads under his togas never could. He inched out on a limb to glimpse the Savior. He risked the shaky-limb experience of faith and responded to the Lord's invitation, not only to come down, but also to grow up.

That day he stepped down from his own efforts to see and be seen and stepped up to the call of the Lord. Zacchaeus still lacked inches, but he gained insight and walked away a giant of a man.

Faith is a believe-it-first proposition, with no promise that I'll get to "see it" regardless of how many boxes I climb. That's scary—like going out on a limb, huh, Zac?

Face-lift

Barbara Johnson

A stranger called me one day and asked if I would like to have a face-lift.

"Who is this again?" I asked, dumbfounded that such a call came from out of the blue. As I spoke, I leaned around the corner so I could peek at my face in the hallway mirror. I puckered my mouth just a little, trying to find my cheekbones.

The woman laughed and said she worked for a plastic surgeon who had just performed a face-lift on a friend of mine. She explained that when the doctor did a face-lift, he offered a big discount to any patient who gave him the names of four friends who might also be interested.

"She . . . she thought I needed a face-lift?" I stuttered, lifting my chin indignantly to smooth out the creases in my neck. "She said I would be interested?"

"Well, uh, I guess she did," the woman said, a little embarrassed when she realized that my friend (*former friend,* I was thinking) hadn't prepared me for her call. "But it sounds like you're not interested, huh?"

"You got *that* right!" I answered. I hung up the phone, trying to decide whether to feel hurt, angry—or old. When I glanced into the hall mirror again, my face had contorted into a disgusted frown. For one brief moment I saw the droopy eyelids, the neck creases, the wrinkles everywhere. Then, just as quickly, I decided to laugh about the whole thing. And what do you know? My face lifted all by itself!

To Bean or Not to Bean

Marilyn Meberg

When Beth and Steve decided to get married in Italy, I realized I would need a coat! This southern California damsel did not even own a winter coat because she rarely needed one. But, I reasoned, if we were all going to traipse to Europe in the dead of winter, do the tourist thing by going to Paris first, and then do the wedding thing, I needed to ward off the potential of freezing to death.

L. L. Bean is a mail-order house in Freeport, Maine, whose catalogs I pore over regularly. I love that place! Almost all of my wool-cashmere blazers have come from there, and my turtlenecks and sweaters as well. There's something irresistibly fun about simply picking up the phone, calling the toll-free number, and chatting with one of their amiable salespersons as I give my order. I always find out how cold it is there and then of course point out that we in southern California are basking in seventy-degree sunshine. (That's an unattractive side of me I'm not proud of, but I seem to continue to express it in spite of my avowed disapproval.)

When my bright-blue quilted goose-down coat with optional zippered hood arrived, I felt ready for any temperature. It claimed to be lightweight for easy packing as well as for wearing, and indeed it was. In fact, it proved so efficiently to retain my body heat, I never once felt cold in spite of freezing temperatures in Paris. I basically just cooed and smiled from the depths of my goose-down cocoon the entire three days we "did" Paris prior to going on to Italy.

Since then, this coat has cuddled and cocooned me many times—sitting on cold bleachers waiting for the Rose Bowl Parade to start, traveling to other cities whose temperatures nearly rival those of wintertime Paris, and then again just last week when we all went to New York for Thanksgiving. (I'd have died without her encompassing warmth while standing rinkside at Rockefeller Center.)

Perhaps now that I have so drawn you into my inordinate affection, as well as appreciation, for "Bean," perhaps you'll understand how startled I was to suddenly realize one morning as we all walked down West 75th Street to Amsterdam Avenue that no one in New York was wearing a bright-blue quilted goose-down coat except me. Everyone was wearing a long black, brown, or tan wool coat. On the heels of this realization came a delayed flashback. I thought, *I don't remember anyone in Paris wearing a bright-blue Bean either.*

I caught my reflection in a window as we hunched our way down Amsterdam Avenue to Sarabeth's for breakfast. *You know, Marilyn, you really look like a walking sleeping bag. I hate to tell you that, but you stick out in a crowd. There* are *no other walking sleeping bags in all of New York!* I was crushed.

After we'd given our breakfast order I turned to my son and said, "Jeff, I want your absolutely honest response. Do you like my coat?"

Jeff stared at me for a minute and then eyeballed the crush of not only my coat but the coats of Pat and Carla on the seat beside me. He said, "You mean the Bean?"

"Yeah, the Bean."

"Well, Mom, because of your happy attachment to her in Paris, I really care only that you continue to be pleased with her."

I looked closely at him to be sure he wasn't doing that Ken Meberg thing. "Jeff, what do you think of my Bean?"

"Mom, uh—she's great for certain places and occasions."

"Jeff, is she good for New York?"

"Probably not, Mom."

"Jeff, was she good for Paris?"

"She kept you warm—but otherwise, no, Mom, she belongs somewhere else."

I looked at my gorgeous, fashion-plate daughter-in-law and said nothing. She too had the grace to say nothing.

My dear friend Pat, whose fidelity to truth-telling is often a challenge to me, offered, "I can tell you the exact place where Bean is appropriate."

Perking up, I asked, "Where?"

"She would be appropriate for you to wear for duck hunting. You know, those places where people lie low and then rise up from the marshes with guns pointed and shoot at ducks who suddenly fly out of nowhere."

I stared at her in total disbelief. "Pat, that's a terrible image. I can't imagine ever lying low to shoot a duck."

"Well, if you change your mind, you've got the coat for it!"

Fortunately, our food arrived, and I settled into my Florentine omelette with extra-crispy bacon on the side. The subject of my Bean didn't come up again.

I must admit there was a slight decrease in my usual ebullience as we went about our activities following breakfast. I was busy settling the Bean issue. So what if I were the only walking bright-blue quilted person in New York, or Paris, or Amboy, California, for that matter! Why do I have to mirror everyone else's subdued earth-tone wool look? I don't! I love my Bean! I'm cozy and warm in my Bean—and as Jeff pointed out, "We can always find you in a crowd!"

What more could one ask from a coat! That settled it: there would be no severing of my relationship with Bean. She stays, and so do I. Nestled beneath several layers of lightweight goose down, I continued our New York activities, secure in the knowledge that I was the only genuinely warm person in the entire city!

Isn't it remarkable how uncomfortable we can become if we don't blend in to our environment? But without God-given uniqueness, everything would look the same, taste the same, and feel the same. What a bore! And what a loss.

Snaggletooth

Luci Swindoll

One of my favorite television commercials has no words. A young woman walks into a shop and admires a bathing suit on a mannequin. With a look of self-satisfaction, she picks up the exact same suit, disappears into a dressing room, and throws her own clothes over the door; after a couple seconds, she lets out a blood-curdling scream. It's a powerhouse endorsement of the diet the commercial recommends. I laugh every time I see it as I munch away on my Snickers bar.

How many times do we look in the mirror and find no words to express what we see? The mirror talks. We scream. Thelma Wells has a good idea. She says, "I'm fully clothed when I look in the mirror 'cause I don't want nuttin' talkin' back to me." Well put.

Recently I had a little screaming fit in front of my bathroom mirror. The dentist had attached a temporary cap on one of my permanent front teeth, which he had earlier filed away to a tiny squared-off yellow stub. That night when I was brushing, the cap fell off into the sink and disappeared down the drain.

At first, with the movement of the toothbrush and a mouthful of toothpaste, I couldn't tell it was gone. I just had a virtual sense of vacancy. Then, running my tongue across my front teeth, I felt nothing more than that stub. The cap was gone. For good. Forever. Forsooth! (Actually, I thought something else, but you don't want to know.)

I smiled into the mirror, then screamed. In short, I panicked. And I rarely panic. Generally I'm very calm, and little makes me lose my cool. But losing my tooth! Well, I lost my cool. I moaned, groaned, whimpered, and wailed. (It's hard to do all that at the same time, but I managed.) I looked in the mirror, hoping a second glance might bring back the tooth, but saw only that awful, gaping hole.

While pacing the hallway, I asked the Lord to take my life. I prayed for the return of Christ. This gaping hole in my mouth was a serious problem. I was leaving at dawn the next morning for Cincinnati, Ohio.

With an unsteady hand I eventually dialed my dentist at home and told him that I had to speak to 15,000 women at a conference that next day and I had no front tooth. I just knew he'd say, "Oh, honey, I understand. You come to the office right now, and I'll fix everything." But he didn't. He promised to meet me the next morning before my flight.

The *next morning?* He might as well have said in my next lifetime! Needless to say, I had a restless night envisioning the most embarrassing moment of my life surrounded by a sea of laughing women.

The next day Dr. Baumann and I both showed up early, and the replacement took place. A very caring, kind man, he looked at me and said (with both fists and several tons of metal in my mouth), "Luci, what if you had to speak with that stub showing? You're still the same person inside, aren't you?"

That'th eathy for you to thay, pal. But you know what? It's true. No matter how different I look on the outside, I'm still me behind the snaggletooth. And I'll be me when I'm completely toothless one day! God, have mercy.

Sometimes the hardest thing in life is being ourselves. We so want to be somebody else. For years I sang with the Dallas Opera chorus, playing the part of other people. It was great. I wore wigs, corsets, fake eyelashes, heavy makeup, and costumes in order to become a waitress or a factory worker, a nun, courtesan, schoolteacher, soldier, witch, dancer, or lady-in-waiting. Whatever was called for, I became that. Interestingly, even my friends in the chorus used to say, "My favorite thing about all this is that I don't have to be me."

The next time you stand in front of a mirror and want to scream, try to remember that *God* made that face. That smile. Those big eyes, crooked teeth, and chubby cheeks. You are his creation, called to reflect him. Spiritual transformation doesn't come from a diet program, a bottle, a makeover, or a mask. It comes from an intimate relationship with the Savior. Because of his gracious nature, he looks beyond our snaggletoothed grin and appreciates us for who we really are. So we can, too.

Look Good, Smell Good!

Chonda Pierce

The other day I read a story about a new suit for men—a scented suit, as a matter of fact. I'm not kidding. They make them in South Korea, and these suits sell for about $400. (Do you know how many pine-tree air fresheners you can buy for that?)

The secret to the suit, I read, are these microscopic capsules implanted in the fabric. These capsules pop open when rubbed or shook to release the scent of lavender, peppermint, or pine. Okay, stop laughing; this is a true story!

I can see where something like this could come in handy. Every time David and I get lost and I make David go into one of those convenience stores to ask for directions, he comes back smelling like Marlboro country. But if he had one of those lavender-scented suits, he could do a little two-step in the parking lot and come wafting back into the car smelling like a butterfly bush. That's when one of those suits would be nice.

But I can think of a few instances in which smelling like a pine tree could be the worst thing—take bears, for instance. That could be dangerous to your health, especially if you're walking through the Smokies one afternoon on your way home from church.

And I don't think I would want to wear one of the lavender-smelling ensembles, either. Not during the heavy periods of cross-pollination (such as the months of April and May)—because of the bee problem.

But what if not only scented *suits* caught on in a big way but also scented clothing of all kinds? Why stop with peppermint, lavender, and pine? Why not take the scented thing as far as it will go? It only makes sense to me.

If you ask people what two things they like the most, many would probably say food and clothes. So why hasn't someone thought of this before? This is a great idea! Children's clothing could be the fun smells of jelly beans, bubble gum, and ice cream. Adults could wear grown-up smells such as fried chicken, okra, and squash (or just meat and potatoes for people like my husband).

Food-scented clothing could help boost sales for some small businesses. For instance, if you sell pizzas and you want to drum up a little extra business, just jump into your pizza-scented coveralls, grab some business cards, and head out to the mall. Waiters could actually wear the soup of the day so, when you ask them, they don't just stand there going, "Ahh ... ahh ... I'm not sure, but I'll find out." They could just sniff their shirtsleeves, and they would know.

Food-scented clothing could help one's self-esteem. I love the smell of popcorn, but I hate the way my feet smell after being hot and sweaty in my sneakers all day. But what if I had popcorn-scented socks? Then, at the end of the day, my feet would smell just like a bowl of Orville Redenbacher's extra-buttery. (Everyone would love me!) And what could be more relaxing than, after wearing my roast-beef-with-gravy pantsuit all day, to come home and slip into my chocolate brownie pajamas?

Dressing for the seasons would be more fun than simply "flannel in the winter and rayon in the summer." On the coldest days, I'd love to wear my chili con carne sweatshirt with my saltine mittens. And on really hot days, I'd wear something fruity, like watermelon or kiwi.

And think of the time food-scented clothing would save, too. Instead of standing in front of the closet every morning and wasting all that time trying to match up colors, I could simply match smells (and plan for supper at the same time).

I know there would be some problems. "You can't wear fish with pasta," someone would say. But look at not only all the different choices that would be available to you but also the combinations. Of course, my husband would be happy to knock around in the ground beef sweatshirt and pants, with cheese socks, pickle

T-shirt, and a ketchup ball cap—smelling like a cheeseburger all day. Me? I'd love to take a gourmet clothing lesson or two and be a different casserole every day—perhaps even a quiche every now and then.

I don't doubt that clothes would still be a marker of status. It would be obvious (without labels) who was wearing the filet mignon skirt and jacket and who was wearing the cheap sirloin skirt and jacket. There would be those who would insist on wearing a caviar camisole or perhaps an escargot dinner jacket, just because they thought they should.

I don't doubt, either, that some fake stuff would be going on, causing us to be more aware of the scams and to watch for imitation crabmeat sweaters, powdered milk blouses, ground turkey slacks—things like that. We would have to be on guard constantly and schooled regularly to distinguish the genuine from the pretend. (Imagine your embarrassment at attending a formal function wearing what you thought was a genuine lamb chop sequined gown only to discover it was some soybean by-product.)

Meeting people would be more than just shaking hands and asking about their jobs. "Oh, I just love the smell of that outfit! What is it? Egg roll? Without MSG, right?" But the downside of this is that complete strangers would stop you to sniff your clothes. "Sorry. I thought I detected the aroma of cabbage stew." (The lesson here is not to borrow someone else's jacket and then embarrass yourself because you don't know the difference between a trout and a salmon.)

And I can imagine the conversations I would have. "Chonda," my friend would call to say, "what are you wearing tonight?"

"Since we're just going out to the mall, I figured I'd wear my black olive slacks and that pimento blouse I showed you the other day."

"Oh, shoot, I was going to wear my pimento top, too, but don't you think that will be too much pimento?"

"Not at all. David's wearing this nifty egg salad sweater that I got him for Christmas, so we should be okay. We'll just make sure he stands between us. What about your husband?"

"Well, he has this pickle thing he could wear."

"Any mayonnaise or cream cheese?"

"Just in dress slacks, but I think he wanted to go a bit more casual. How about mustard boxers?"

"Perfect."

Food-scented clothing may be the best idea since the Y2K-scare books. (I wish I had invented those.) It will encourage us to love our neighbor more. (I've stood in line next to people I could have loved a whole lot more if they had just smelled like a Salisbury steak.) And I believe food-scented clothing will also help people to lose weight. I mean, if you walk around all day smelling like meat loaf, the last thing you're going to dig into is a fatty meat loaf recipe that night. (If your weakness is bratwurst, the same thing holds true.)

Going to the mall would be like going to Luby's Cafeteria. Going to Luby's Cafeteria would be like going to Sak's Fifth Avenue. Food and clothes, clothes and food—together at last. Life would be good!

But I was just wondering: Will I need more closet space, or a bigger refrigerator?

Big Hair Day

Cathy Lee Phillips

It was a big hair day. I made that decision on a whim, little knowing the events it would set into motion. This was a few years ago, when "big" hair was in style and I had just received a new perm in my auburn (absolutely no gray, of course!) locks. Because my curls were shoulder length, I occasionally used a variety of accessories to corral my hair into a sleek ponytail or other various styles. However, on this particular day I opted for the tousled, carefree, "big hair" look—a decision I would live to regret. I finished the style with half a bottle of Mega Spritz, a gluelike spray that provided my big hair the power to withstand a hurricane.

My husband and I were in a hurry that morning. Jerry was flying to Colorado Springs, Colorado, for a convention of the United Methodist Association of Church Business Administrators. I would fight the Atlanta traffic going toward the airport, drop Jerry off in time to catch his flight, and then fight more traffic to reach my office on the other side of Atlanta.

My schedule that day was quite full—it included a lunch appointment and several afternoon meetings. Leaving my office that afternoon, I fought more traffic, ran a gazillion errands, met friends for dinner, and returned home well after 11:00 that dark night.

Though I was completely exhausted, I was proud that my big hair sill looked fresh, thanks to its three-inch glaze of Mega Spritz.

Crawling into bed that night, I was almost asleep when I realized I had forgotten one very important task. Rhett and Ashley were two beautiful cocker spaniels—one black and one blonde—who did not want to suffer hunger pangs all night long. Feeding them was normally Jerry's job, but he had safely arrived in Colorado and had no intention of flying home to feed two cocker spaniels, no matter how special they were.

"Those two dogs will surely live until morning," I rationalized, "and they could actually stand to lose a pound or two." I snuggled deeper under the covers and punched the pillow into a comfortable position.

I tried to sleep, but the faces of those two lovable old dogs appeared each time I closed my eyes. I was warm and comfortable and did not want to crawl out of bed. But there was a bigger issue at stake.

I, Cathy Lee Phillips, am afraid of the dark. I grew up where there was talk of boogers and monsters and haints and such—a virtual smorgasbord of creatures just waiting to grab and torment me in the night. *(A word of explanation may be necessary for the Yankees or the very young among us:* Haint *is an old Southern word meaning anything scary, frightening, or just generally creepy.)* Though talk of these creatures took place during my childhood, I remained convinced that boogers and monsters and haints still awaited me in the dark.

So, while I was warm and comfortable in bed that night, I basically did not want to face the terrors of the dark. But my love for these old dogs prevailed, and I reluctantly climbed out of bed, pulled a purple chenille robe over my still perfect big hair, and slipped my feet inside my Nikes.

What a picture I was that midnight—a weirdly dressed, scared-of-the-dark, big-haired preacher's wife facing boogers and monsters and haints to undertake a mission of mercy for two beloved cocker spaniels.

Rhett and Ashley lived in a "doggie condo" behind our parsonage. Inside their fence was a shed that housed them, a riding mower, assorted junk, and an ample supply of Wal-Mart Old Roy dog food. It also housed an abundance of flies, quite possibly attracted to the halo of Mega Spritz encircling our house.

What I did not know—and what Jerry failed to tell me before he boarded his flight that morning—was that the shed also housed something else that dark night. You see, my dear husband decided to tackle the problem of those pesky flies with an age-old remedy—yes, flypaper. About two inches wide, the flypaper came in little canisters that hooked to the roof of the building and hung approximately three feet from the ceiling. The desired effect, of course, was that flies and mosquitoes would innocently crash into this sticky substance where they would remain until their bodies became lifeless.

Jerry, I must say, was *very* efficient when it came to dealing with annoying flying creatures and was not content to simply suspend one or two strips of flypaper. No! He virtually covered the ceiling of that little shed with a truckload of sticky strips hanging down several feet.

As I bent down to open the plastic container of Wal-Mart Old Roy dog food, I luckily avoided the flypaper. But as I stood up straight (all five feet zero inches of me), my big hair felt a tug. My head was pulled backwards, and I was suddenly encased in something unknown and very sinister. In the eerie darkness I did not realize that it was me, not the mosquitoes, that the flypaper had captured so skillfully.

Sections of flypaper seized my big hair, while others slapped at my face. The harder I fought, the harder my unknown enemy fought back. The flypaper seized my hair and the fuzzy material of my chenille robe. It stuck to me as I flailed my arms and bravely battled the boogers and monsters and haints I vividly envisioned. My heart pounded as I shrieked, and with great effort I finally broke free from the invisible enemy tormenting me. I raced toward the safety of the parsonage, where I slammed and bolted the door and tried to breathe normally again. Running to the bathroom, I faced my reflection in the large mirror. It was *not* a pretty sight. Staring back at me was a terrorized preacher's wife complete with Tammy Faye mascara running from my panic-stricken eyes, while my big hair looked as though it had been brushed in a blender and dipped in Mega Spritz and flypaper.

It was well past 3:00 A.M. before my heart stopped pounding and the final remnants of flypaper were pulled from my big hair.

While I have never looked a roll of flypaper in the face again, I still have days when terror and darkness grip my heart. There is much to fear in our imperfect world. My advice for handling those fearful moments? Boldly face those days with your hair small and your faith big, and walk confidently with a loving God who understands your anxiety and gently whispers, "Fear not!"

CHAPTER SIX

Nothing to Do but Laugh: Life's Most Embarrassing Moments

Man is the only animal that blushes.
Or needs to.
—Mark Twain

The problem with people
is that they're only human.
—Calvin and Hobbes

Slippery Slope

Betty Malz

I had driven three hours with my friend Gloria Hutchens to speak at Sauk Center, Minnesota, for a Saturday night church rally. It was November 6—my birthday. We arrived there only ten minutes before I was to be introduced. While Gloria went to tell the pastor that we had made it, I went downstairs to the rest room. As usual, the ladies' room was full—and about twenty women were waiting in the hallway. The men's room was empty. I figured I'd temporarily claim the territory, so I slipped in. No one had seen me, and no one would ever know.

Well, they had recently remodeled the rest room and had covered the cement steps that led up to the "white throne" with a very slick gray porcelain-finish paint. Although I stepped carefully, I whacked my head on the overhead plumbing. I winced and felt a painful knot on my head, but I knew it would be all right. But when I started up the steps, my high wooden heels slipped. My feet went out from under me, and I cracked the back of my head on that cement. When I woke up, I was at the bottom of the steps. My back now hurt more than my head, and my belt was broken. I could hear the congregation singing upstairs. I could not see my feet, and soon I realized that the heels of my shoes had run right through a plasterboard wall and were protruding into the hallway in the dust of white, chalky powder.

I heard two men talking in the hall. One said, "What is this?" The other opened the door and answered, "I believe it's our speaker." "Not anymore," the first one remarked. "She'll never make it. She may be a writer, but she can't read." Then he called out, "Do you know you're in the men's room?"

"Yes," I muttered, although I didn't see what difference that made at this point in the game.

Then came the second dumb question. "Are you hurt?"

I couldn't help but reply, "No, I'm not hurt. I always exit the rest room this way."

I was determined I was going to speak. I assured them I would be okay, put my broken belt in my purse, and struggled to the platform. Somehow I got through the evening, but the pastor could tell that something was wrong. After the rally, when I told him my story, he wouldn't believe me until he'd gone to check it out for himself. You should have heard the roar!

All the way home that night I moaned. I couldn't sleep, and the next day the doctor told me I'd broken my tailbone—snapped off the last three tiny bones at the end of my spine. I didn't even try to explain the accident to the doctor.

Weeks later I got a letter from the pastor's secretary telling me that they didn't repair the hole but posted a sign that read, "Betty Malz was here."

Looking back now, the whole story is hilariously funny, and I can laugh about it. But, as the psalmist said, I had to endure the night of weeping before I was able to experience the joy that comes in the morning.

A River Runs Down It

Charlene Ann Baumbich

For Christmas last year, my son, Bret, gave me a wonderful and very useful gift: a fanny pack (to balance my built-in fanny pack) that is able to hold a drink bottle. Since I am, undoubtedly, Queen of the Perpetual Drink Sippers, that was, indeed, a handy item.

Before my husband, George, and I left on our annual trek to the local county fair, I filled 'er up and strapped 'er on. After walking around for about an hour and finishing my second tankful, so to speak, it was time to hit the john. Right now!

Since it was a very hot, sticky day and since a strapped-on fanny pack makes loosening clothing so much more difficult, I unsnapped it from around my waist and hung it around my neck so I could negotiate the necessities without impairment.

In the nick of time, I was free to do my duty. Whew! But by midstream, a horrible sensation struck me. In the heat and desperateness of disencumbering myself from the tacky clothes, I must not have gotten something pulled down right. To make it worse, it was beyond my capabilities to shut off the tap, so to speak. I was stunned, humiliated, and wet.

Then the light dawned. I hadn't secured the pop-up top on the drink bottle dangling from my neck. Although my shorts were a mess, I was relieved to find out that the situation wasn't what I had first believed it to be.

But relief was brief, because suddenly I saw them—the dancing feet of the lady in the stall next to me. The stream of water that had run down my leg had quickly flowed in her direction. Of course, she didn't know that the stream had originated from my water bottle, so I quickly hollered, "It's not what you think! It's my water bottle."

My reassurance did nothing to stop those dancing feet that were trying to hover, one at a dancing time, above the floor and out of the stream.

I exited the stall before her and dutifully waited to show her exactly what had happened. I had become nearly hysterical with laughter by this point.

When the lady exited her stall, I tried, accompanied by my own peals of laughter, to give her a quick demo as to what had happened. She didn't laugh, she didn't smile, she didn't wash her hands. She simply left me standing there alone, wearing wet pants and babbling and laughing.

The next lady who entered the bathroom took a swift up-and-down look at me, and she didn't laugh, either.

Dear Lord, thanks for helping me to laugh at myself. Especially when I'm the only one who thinks I'm funny. Okay, so the joke's on me, but at least I get it!

Gourmet Goodies

Patsy Clairmont

My friend Lana learned some lessons about exactitude when her son's girlfriend invited her for a birthday dinner. It turns out this gal was a gourmet cook, and Lana said it was one of the best meals she had ever eaten. Everything had been prepared exactly as it should have been.

Lana's only disappointment was that some of her good friends didn't get to sample this excellent fare.

So Lana was elated when a second invitation arrived to attend an open house and to bring guests of her choice—exactly what Lana had hoped for, gourmet goodies and all. Lana regaled her friends about this dream-come-true cook.

When they arrived, Lana and her enthusiastic friends gathered in the living room and selected cozy seats around a tray of lovely appetizers. Eager to sample them, Lana's guest Beverly selected an item and dipped it into the candle-heated sauce. She took a bite, chewed, and swallowed—and then began to spit. She tried to dispose of the rest of her gourmet treat into her napkin while shaking her head in disgust.

Lana was aghast. "What's wrong?" she whispered to her friend.

"It's terrible," Beverly choked out quietly.

"Don't be silly," Lana replied, beginning to feel defensive. Then to prove her friend wrong, Lana picked up the identical item, dipped it into the sauce, and popped it into her mouth. Her eyes began to grow larger, and she looked for a place to get rid of the disgusting stuff lodged in her burning mouth. Her now-experienced friend handed her some napkins. Lana was confused, embarrassed, and nauseated.

She decided the offending culprit was something in the raspberry sauce. When one of the kitchen helpers walked through the room, Lana meekly asked about the sauce's contents.

"Sauce?" said the woman. "Why, that's liquid potpourri!"

Later Lana had to admit the evening hadn't exactly gone as she thought it would. The good news? Lana and Beverly had the sweetest breath for weeks afterward!

Putting on the Ritz

Cathy Lee Phillips

The Ritz Carlton? Well, maybe I can adjust my schedule."

The rat! For several weeks I had been begging Jennifer to go to the beach with me, but a variety of scheduling conflicts had kept her close to home. So, being an independent woman of the world, I decided to go by myself. *I've been to college and I hold a steady job,* I thought. *I certainly can go to the beach by myself.*

I called my travel agent with my criteria: I wanted to practically roll out of the bed and onto the beach. And I wanted something relatively close to my hometown. I didn't want to spend my entire vacation driving to and from my destination.

Within the hour my travel agent called back. "Have I got a deal for you," she practically shouted with excitement. "In fact, if you don't take this, I will."

The Ritz Carlton, Amelia Island, Florida. They were offering a special rate of $159 per night for a suite that normally rented for $650 per night. The Ritz Carlton! I had never visited a Ritz before, but I knew of their reputation for being the ultimate in pampering and luxury.

"Book it!" I told my travel agent.

Next, I called Jennifer to gloat. She was my best friend, a fellow PW (Preacher's Wife), with a temperament so like mine it was frightening. Most people thought we were sisters because of our similar looks and personality. Of course, because I had no gray hair, people naturally thought I was the younger sister.

Our husbands pastored neighboring United Methodist churches in Cherokee County, Georgia. Therefore, we saw each other often at community and church events. We quickly became close friends. Jennifer was a teacher, with a long summer vacation, so it seemed sensible that she could accompany me to the beach. But her summer calendar filled quickly that year. It seemed that she had no time for pitiful little me—until I mentioned the Ritz Carlton. Like me, she only knew of the Ritz by reputation and couldn't pass up the chance to spend a few days in this luxury resort.

In short, Jennifer somehow changed her plans, and on a hot July afternoon, these two preacher's wives from Cherokee County turned toward the beach. Over the six-hour drive we talked and laughed like two teenagers at a slumber party. We sang along with the radio and even played word games to pass the time.

As we neared the island, however, we began to think seriously about something important to both of us snacks! We were on vacation; everyone knows that calories do not count while you are on vacation. We had no idea what edibles the hotel would offer, so we made a quick stop at a convenience store for the basics:

√ Two cases of caffeine-free Diet Coke
√ DoubleStuf Oreos
√ Cheese and crackers
√ Cherry Pop Tarts for breakfast
√ One bag of Almond Joy candy bars
√ An oversize bag of bright-orange cheese puffs
√ One disposable razor, because Jennifer had forgotten to shave her legs

In our old shorts and tank tops we made quite a scene as we raided the convenience store. We paid in cash so no one would know our names.

We arrived at Amelia Island about twenty minutes later and looked for signs to the Ritz Carlton. Distracted by our chatter, we missed the turn. Realizing we were lost, we decided to head toward the water—since the hotel was on the beachfront. We would find it eventually. In the distance we spotted a large hotel with a beautiful blue roof and turned toward it.

"I'd like to stay at a place like that just once before I die," Jennifer remarked. Hoping we might find the Ritz in the general area of that beautiful building, we drove toward it. As we approached, we finally saw the signs that would direct us to the Ritz Carlton. Making one last turn, we suddenly discovered that the large hotel with the blue roof *was* actually the Ritz Carlton!

I stopped the car just short of the entrance.

"I feel completely outclassed," I whispered, looking at my old shorts and tank top. And Jennifer still had not shaved her legs. Not knowing what else to do, I shifted the car into drive and slowly approached the hotel.

An army of uniformed attendants descended upon the car. "Welcome to the Ritz Carlton. May we get your bags? Please let me valet-park your car while you check in. Did you have a pleasant trip?"

Walking inside, Jennifer and I surveyed the tall ceilings, the ornate furnishings, the fresh flowers, and the strict attention to detail. Just then a nicely dressed bellman brought our luggage cart into the lobby. Glancing over, I realized that the oversized bag of cheese puffs had pushed through the top of our brown bag of snacks. The bag rustled loudly as the cart moved.

I wanted to register under an alias!

Jennifer, meanwhile, used the "I think I'll stand off to the side and pretend I don't know her" approach. After all, the room was reserved in my name, and no one even knew that Jennifer Huycke existed.

Laugh on, Jennifer, I thought to myself. *At least my legs are freshly shaven!*

The bellman led us to our accommodations on the sixth floor. The foyer opened into a suite that was easily larger than my first apartment. The sitting room was beautifully decorated in tones of green, with an overstuffed sofa and chairs and a large color television. A separate bedroom was equally posh, with two queen beds, desks, and a tall armoire holding another large television. An immense hallway held two large closets, complete with thick terry cloth Ritz Carlton robes. There was also a safe for our valuables (maybe the cheese puffs?). A large private balcony overlooked the beach and a perfectly manicured courtyard. Three separate marble bathrooms completed the ensemble.

"Are your accommodations suitable, Mrs. Phillips?" the bellman asked.

"Perfectly," I replied.

When he left the room, Jennifer and I squealed with delight. The place was gorgeous—and it was ours for the next three days!

"Where is the phone!" Jennifer shrieked. "I have to call Dick and tell him about this place!"

We looked around the suite and found a variety of phones—six in all. Choosing one on a table next to the sofa, Jennifer remarked, "Wow, look at all the buttons on this phone. I wonder what they all do."

"Just don't call Alaska or do anything to embarrass me," I instructed, remembering that the registration was in my name only.

Lifting the receiver, Jennifer punched in a series of numbers that connected her with the parsonage in Cherokee County. Dick was not home, but in our excitement we proceeded to leave a very long and very silly message describing our arrival at the Ritz Carlton. With great animation we related everything—from the uniformed attendants meeting our car to the orange bag of cheese puffs gliding through the lobby on our luggage cart. Jennifer described the room in detail—from the posh furnishings to the magnificent view.

While she talked, I explored the suite and found, to my amazement, that each bathroom was equipped with a telephone. It hung on the wall next to the toilet. So as Jennifer continued to babble, I picked up the extension from the bathroom in the foyer and said, "Hey, Dick, I am using the phone in the bathroom. Just think, I can go to the bathroom and talk to you at the same time. This phone is in bathroom number one. You don't believe me? Well, I'll prove it."

And I held the receiver at an angle that would pick up the sound of the toilet as I flushed it. Continuing with this theme, I walked into the next bathroom.

"Hello, Dick. I am in bathroom number two. It has a gray marbled floor, a large tub, and a mirror that covers the whole wall. And guess what? There is a phone next to this toilet, too! Just listen."

And I flushed toilet number two.

"Dick, this is me in bathroom number three. We have another marble floor and a shower with a glass door. There are tons of towels and Ritz Carlton toiletries. And, of course, there is a phone. Listen to this!"

And I flushed toilet number three.

Jennifer and I were red-faced by the time we completed our bizarre message. We were having a great time!

"Now, I've just got to call Mom," and Jennifer again began pushing buttons on the large phone. Before the connection was made, however, she stopped, turned pale as a ghost, and placed the receiver on the base.

"What?" I demanded. "What's wrong?"

For a few brief seconds she was completely quiet, still pale. Then she spoke in a subdued voice.

"Someone from the hotel office spoke to me when I began dialing," she relayed. "I could hear giggling in the background as they gave me some phone instructions."

"What instructions?" I practically shouted.

Still pale and obviously horrified, Jennifer said, "They told me that I should depress the conference-call button before I made my next call. And they called me *Mrs. Phillips.*"

This could mean only one thing: the staff in the hotel office had heard our entire ridiculous, absurd, laughable conversation. I turned pale myself. Jennifer was obviously telling the truth. I knew she was—she would *never* have used the word "depress." She would have used "push" or "press," instead. She's a kindergarten teacher, after all!

For me, the most awful part of this nightmare was that the operator had called her *Mrs. Phillips.* The Ritz Carlton did not know Jennifer at all; they only knew that the room was registered to *Mrs. Phillips.* They even knew my home address and my credit card number.

"I'm never leaving this room," I said, completely humiliated.

Jennifer confessed, "I think I want to go home."

Silence filled the room—at least for a few minutes—until Jennifer began a soft giggle that quickly matured into a loud belly laugh. It took me a few minutes longer to see the humor in the situation, because I was, after all, *Mrs. Phillips*—the registered guest.

We laughed until our sides hurt. We laughed until we rolled off the sofa and onto the dark green carpets. We laughed until tears rolled down our faces. We laughed until we each had to use one of the three bathrooms in the suite.

The Trouble with Peanuts

Barbara Johnson

Recently someone sent me a silly story about a preacher who visited an elderly woman from his congregation. As they talked, he nibbled from a bowl of peanuts on the coffee table. They visited for nearly an hour, and by the time the preacher was ready to leave, he had eaten the whole bowl of peanuts. A little embarrassed, he told the woman, "I have to apologize. I really just meant to nibble a few peanuts."

"Oh, that's okay," the old lady reassured him. "Ever since I lost my teeth all I can do is suck the chocolate off them anyway."

CHAPTER SEVEN

Raising Laughs: Humor and Parenting

*Parents are the last people on earth
who ought to have children.*
—Samuel Butler

*Oh, what a tangled web do parents weave
when they think that their children are naive.*
—Ogden Nash

Bare Witness

Phil Callaway

It's BATH NIGHT. Around the world hurried and harried parents seize precious moments to rest and recharge while their children set uncontested Olympic records in the dunking and "I got more water on the walls and ceiling than you did" events.

At our peculiar house on this particular night, a four-year-old and his younger brother are all wet. The older is constructing a bubble bath beard on the younger. I can't help overhearing their conversation:

"Did you know that you've done bad things?"

"Yeah." It is one of three words one-year-old Jeffrey knows. The other two are "yep" and "uh-huh."

"You have done sins," continues the four-year-old kindly.

"Yep."

"And you shall go to hell."

"Yep."

"Hell is hot."

The one-year-old is making a hole in the soap bar.

"But you can go to heaven. Do you want to go to heaven?"

Jeffrey sips some bathwater before responding: "Uh-huh."

"Then ask Jesus into your heart."

"Yeah."

"I'll pray for you, okay?"

"Yep."

Moments later an excited four-year-old stands before his parents—dripping wet, wearing a smile. "Daddy! Mommy! Guess what?"

"What, Stephen?"

"Jeffrey asked Jesus into his heart."

Jeffrey is one. You might say that he's a baby Christian.

"Rachael!" A few days have passed since Stephen claimed his first trophy. He is on a roll, and he isn't about to stop now. Especially at mealtimes. "Did you know that you've done bad things?"

"No." It is two-year-old Rachael's most common response.

"You have done sins," the four-year-old continues, undaunted.

"Haven't." Rachael is trying to stab a pea with a fork.

"Yes, you have."

"No. Haven't . . . "

"YES!"

"NO!"

"YEEEEEESS YOU HAVE!" The witnesser throws part of a sesame seed bun at the witnessee. The bun misses. There are sesame seeds everywhere.

"All right, Stephen. Come with me."

Down the hall we go, hand in hand. He is unsure of the consequences. I can't think of a thing to say. Kneeling down, I hold him tight. Ah, my son. The bare witness. "Don't throw things at your sister."

"Okay," he says, and he wiggles free. "One more thing," I say, as he disappears around the corner. "You will sweep up those sesame seeds."

Evening has come. The children are tucked in. Mom is out with my VISA card, and I am in bed reading. A little pajama-clad figure with bare feet slowly pokes his head around the corner. "Hi," he says.

"Stephen, you should be asleep." My tone is unconvincing. He knows his father is a softy when it comes to bedtime.

"What are you eating?"

"Grapes."

"Are they good?"

"Come here and see." I pull down the covers, and he crawls in. Grapes are better shared.

"What are you reading?" he asks, looking at the book I'm holding—a best-seller I don't read enough.

"It's the Bible. Do you want me to read to you?"

"Yep."

"I'm reading from a book called Matthew. Remember the song you like, 'I don't wanna be a Pharisee, 'cause they're not fair you see'? Well, one of the Pharisees asked Jesus what he wanted him to do most of all. Do you know what Jesus said?"

"What?"

"He told him to love God with everything he had—and do you know what else?"

"What?"

"He told him to love others like he loved himself. Don't you think it's more important to love others than to tell them about Jesus? You've been telling Rachael and Jeffrey about Jesus, and that makes me glad. But they need to see how kind you are to them before they'll believe what you say about Jesus. Love them, Stephen. Grown-up Christians like to talk about *contacts* and *souls*. Sometimes we sort of throw buns, too, but we don't talk very often about loving those who don't know Jesus. We need to love people so they begin to ask us why."

My son has been silent. Undoubtedly, he's impressed with my verbose rhetoric. I mean, let's face it. This has been pretty good stuff. I look over at him. His mouth is wide-open, but not with awe. He is sound asleep. Perhaps all this advice was really meant for me.

Good Grief!

Karen Scalf Linamen

When Kaitlyn turned eleven, she wanted one thing and one thing only for her birthday. Pet rats. I didn't ask my husband, Larry, what he thought about the idea. After all, there are just some things for which it's easier to obtain forgiveness than permission. Instead, I peeled open the Yellow Pages and looked under pets—and before you could say, "Mouse droppings," Cecelia and Megan had come to live with us.

They were adorable, all white and inquisitive and good-natured. The little ladies had been a part of our family for about a week when I looked into their glass cage and noticed something tiny and pink wiggling next to Cecelia. I blinked. Stared. Blinked again. It was a baby rat. I called the pet store. The woman on the other end of the line sounded puzzled. "She must have been pregnant when she left here, although I didn't think either of those rats were nearly old enough. And I'm amazed there's only one baby. I've never heard of a rat giving birth to a litter of just one. Oh well. Think of it as a two-for-one special. Or maybe three-for-two. However you count 'em, congratulations and good luck."

Kacie, then two and a half, bonded immediately with the baby. Forget watching *Rugrats*—Kacie watched our own rats and daily monitored the progress of our tiny guest.

Everything was going great until one morning I looked into the nest and discovered that the baby rat had died during the night.

My biggest concern was how to tell Kacie. Larry and I discussed it at length. I voted for the straightforward approach, but

Larry wondered if Kacie was too young to understand the idea of death—and in the end I agreed.

You know that old saying "what a tangled web we weave"? Well, I started weaving the very afternoon the baby rat died. After disposing of the tiny body, I pulled Kacie onto my lap and gently explained that the baby rat had simply "gone away." This was my first mistake. "Gone where? Who took it out of the cage? Does Cecelia know it's gone? Did it walk, or go in a car? Where did it go? When is it coming back? Who's going to feed it while it's gone? Is it visiting its family? Is Cecelia sad the baby's gone? Can we go find the baby?"

I tried to answer all her questions. But in my attempt to protect her, I tried to answer her questions without actually giving her any accurate information. This, of course, led to more questions, and one thing led to another until . . . Two hours later, I called my mom in a panic. "I don't think I handled this very well," I explained. "I started off nice and vague, but Kacie bombarded me with so many questions that I guess I got a little carried away, and now, well, now she thinks the baby took a train to rat heaven. She's roaming the house, yelling, 'Baby rat, where are you?' trying to convince it to catch the 6:15 back home. This has gotten entirely out of hand."

When my mother responded, I could hear the smile in her voice. "Karen, it's simple. Here's what you need to do and say . . . " I followed her instructions to the letter. My conversation with Kacie went without a hitch. I pulled the tiny body from the trash and let Kacie see and even touch the lifeless form (thank God for antibacterial soap!). I chose my words carefully when explaining how the baby rat had died. I didn't want to say the little rat had fallen asleep and would never wake up—what if Kacie became afraid to fall asleep herself? I didn't want to say the mother forgot to feed it— what if Kacie missed a meal and began to fear for her life? No, I had to pick a cause of death that had no easily identifiable counterpart in Kacie's world.

I told her the mother rat sat on the baby. I rarely, if ever, sit on my children, so this was probably a pretty safe choice.

I suggested we bury the baby in the backyard, but Kacie wasn't ready for that quite yet. It took three days of talking and looking and touching before she was ready to say good-bye. Then we took the baby rat into the backyard and buried it under a cedar tree. This was Kacie's first encounter with death.

Awhile later Larry's grandmother died. When we heard the news, we packed up our van and drove from Texas to Arizona to be with other family members as we grieved the loss, remembered the legacy, and celebrated the life of Eyla Linamen.

Of course, this also meant that I found myself with yet another opportunity to talk to Kacie about loss. Thankfully, Kacie was nearly four years old by now and had matured a little since our tiny pet took the train to rat heaven.

I thought about calling my mom again for advice. But Kacie wasn't the only one who had developed since the untimely passing of Baby Rat. I had learned a thing or two myself, and I was ready to handle this one on my own.

For just a heartbeat I wondered whether Kacie would be traumatized or comforted by viewing her great-grandmother's body. Then, remembering Cecelia's dear departed baby, Larry and I agreed that a straightforward, concrete approach was the best path.

We let Kacie view the body, which she found intriguing. Then I sat down with her on a sofa in the foyer of the funeral home and tried to explain what she had just observed. This is what I said:

"Kacie, yesterday you played all day, didn't you? You ran and played and got all dirty and messy. And at the end of the day, you needed to take a bath, so you went into your room, took off all your clothes, and ran naked into the bathroom. When that happened, you were in one room and your clothes were in another. Could your clothes run and play anymore? Could they move all by themselves? Of course not. They lay crumbled on the floor, worn and discarded, unable to stir or shift or move by themselves. But you weren't crumpled on the floor, were you? You were in the other room, naked, laughing, and playing in the water.

"That's what happened to Great-Grandma. That's what will happen to all of us one day. Our bodies are like clothes. We wear them for a while. We run and play, and after a while our bodies get wrinkled and worn. And when they're pretty much worn-out, Jesus helps us to climb out of them. He lets us leave them crumpled on the floor, and we run on into heaven. That's where Great-Grandma is. Her body is here, but she's in heaven."

Kacie thought for a moment. I knew I was in trouble when she said, matter-of-factly, "So Great-Grandma is naked in heaven?"

"Yes, well," I hedged, "I don't think she's still naked. I think God gave her another body to wear. You know, kind of like when you put on pajamas after your bath."

Kacie looked at her body and tugged at the skin on her arm. Then she looked at me. "How did Great-Grandma take off her body? I don't know how to take off my body. Can I climb out of my body, too?"

"Um, not exactly. We can't do it ourselves. Jesus has to help us. Only he knows when our bodies are worn enough and it's time for a new one."

"But how?"

"How?"

"How does Jesus do it?"

"Do what?" I was stalling for time.

"Get our bodies off us?" I had no choice; I had to tell her.

That afternoon, Kacie ran to Larry's dad, climbed into his lap, and asked loudly, "Grandpa, did you know that God unzipped Great-Grandma's body? Great-Grandma's body has an invisible zipper."

Dad blinked. "A zipper?"

"Yep. Everybody's does. We don't know where it is, so we can't unzip it ourselves. Only God knows about the zipper."

"I didn't know that."

"Yep. And do you know what happened then?"

"I can't say that I do."

Kacie's eyes widened with excitement as she leaned in close and blurted, "Great-Grandma ran naked into heaven!"

Perhaps I should have called my mother for advice after all.

Bite My Tongue!

Sue Buchanan

From the time Dana was born, we prayed that she would marry the right person someday and that it would be God's choice, not ours. It took Dana a long time to show even the slightest interest in boys. She was a late bloomer. By the time she was in eleventh grade, we'd pretty much pegged her as antisocial and slightly boring. Yes, I know she is my very own daughter and that's a cruel thing to say, but sometimes a mother has to face facts.

Then, in her senior year, she discovered the harp, and suddenly she was known. She was in demand to play at every event—talent shows and musicals, and she even became a member of the Nashville Youth Symphony. One night when she returned from a rehearsal—we always waited up to help her unload, lamenting the fact she hadn't chosen to play a piccolo—she had with her the cutest, tallest, most muscular, blond-haired boy you ever laid eyes on. Balanced on one of his shoulders was the harp. Heretofore, it had taken the three of us to manipulate it out of the station wagon, into the house, and up the stairs. *Whoosh,* went the wind out of Wayne's sails, when he realized that he might never be needed again. If for no other reason than that, we knew this boy couldn't possibly be the one.

After the blond Adonis came a total opposite: a dark, fun-loving Jewish boy, and we all fell in love, especially Wayne after he discovered David couldn't move the harp by himself. My guess is, knowing David, that even if he could have, he was smart enough to play the game.

It wasn't unusual for Dana and David to come home late after a date and barge right into our room, ready to entertain us with their evening's adventures. It was fun while it lasted. We knew deep down that David wasn't the one; his background was very Jewish, and Dana's was very Christian. Each recognized that their heritage was part of who they were, and neither intended to change.

In college Dana met Barry, and it didn't take long for us to figure out that this was the one! Watching the two of them together was like watching six-year-olds who simply took delight in each other's presence. Barry's parents, Bonnie and Miles, whom we'd met and fallen in love with, were having the same thoughts we had: these two were meant for each other. In our minds, Bonnie and I were planning a wedding. We chose the colors for our dresses, for heaven's sake!

The problem was that Dana and Barry didn't cooperate! Dana assured us that they could *never* date; they were best friends. "Almost like brother and sister," she said. They graduated from college with no wedding in sight.

Every year, Dana and Barry and their other best friends, Deba and Cary (also not a couple), took a vacation together. Throughout the year, they would visit each other: Barry would come to Nashville, or she would go to Middletown, Ohio. They dated other people, and if he broke up with someone, she was by his side to comfort him. If she broke up with someone, Barry was there, hugging, patting, consoling.

Looked like love to me, but what do I know? I'm just the mother.

Once when I was planning a business trip to Columbus, Ohio, Dana insisted that, instead of flying, I should drive so she could go with me. The plan would be to drop her off in Middletown on the way and pick her up on the way back. Things went according to plan. I dropped her off, continued on to Columbus for a couple of days, did my work, and returned to the designated meeting place in Middletown—the Bob Evans restaurant. They were there, and I pulled in next to them. And I waited. I waited and waited and waited!

When I glanced their way, I could see they were in heavy conversation. I waited!

Even though I tried to keep my glances at a minimum, I couldn't help but notice after a while that Dana was becoming more and more animated. Not in a good way. I knew my daughter well, and I recognized "not in a good way" when I saw it. I waited!

For forty-five minutes I waited, and at last Dana jumped out, slammed the door, threw her duffel bag in the backseat of my car, slammed the door, jumped in the front seat, and slammed that door.

"Go!" she ordered. "Go!" She didn't look back. She didn't wave. And there was certainly no sisterly kiss blown through the breeze—the kind you would expect to see when best friends part.

The look on her face was the look you save for someone who just killed your pet parakeet. She was steaming! Smoke was coming out of her nostrils.

I bit my tongue!

"The nerve of him," she said. "You'll never believe it! You will *never in a million years* believe it!"

I bit my tongue.

"Mother, I am so mad!" she said. "He loves me." It was like she'd just been proposed to by the Ayatollah! She slapped the dashboard for punctuation.

I bit my tongue.

"He's loved me for years. Can you believe it?"

I bit my tongue.

"Know what he said? He said he wants to get married, but he can't wait for me forever." She slapped the dashboard.

"He says he'll have to find someone else if I won't marry him. Can you believe that?" Another slap on the dashboard.

I bit my tongue.

"'Of course, find someone!' I told him. 'Of course, get married! We're just best friends. Always were, always will be.'"

There was a moment of silence, followed by another slap on the dashboard. I noticed that her poor hand was bright-red from the trauma.

As for me, I was thinking I could taste blood running down my throat as a result of my tongue biting! I wondered if the emergency room in the next town was equipped to handle severe carpal tunnel syndrome and tongue biting trauma.

"I'll tell you one thing, though," she said, eyes flashing. The dashboard punctuation was now coming with every word she expelled. "*Whoever* he marries better understand our relationship!"

I could contain myself no longer. I burst out laughing. I'd just taken a mouthful of iced tea, and I spewed it all over me, the dashboard, and the windshield.

"*What!*" she screeched like a banshee, her face now between me and the road, presenting another problem that might end in the trauma center.

"I can promise you," I said, "whoever he marries *won't* understand the relationship."

It was quiet the rest of the way home.

The friendship somehow continued—unchanged as far as I could tell. In the fall, Dana told us that Barry had a girlfriend. In October, she asked us if we could get a ticket for the girl for Praise Gathering. We agreed, and Dana made arrangements for us to meet up with her at our hotel. Just before we left for Indianapolis, Dana phoned.

"Call me as soon as you meet her, and tell me what she's like. Barry Shafer deserves the best. In fact, he deserves *perfect*. This girl needs to be perfect."

Somehow our plans for the meeting went awry, and we never laid eyes on the girl. We ended up leaving her ticket at the desk. When we arrived home, Dana was on our doorstep.

"So what's she like? Is she witty and clever? And fun? Barry's the funnest person in the world. He needs somebody fun. Does she love the Lord? Nobody loves the Lord more than Barry Shafer. Is she cute? Is she pretty? Is she right for Barry?"

Wayne and I were ready! "Oh, I don't know," I said, taking my time. "I guess you could say she's"—I'm milking it for all its worth—"she's cuddly." Wayne shook his head in agreement.

"Cuddly? CUDDLY?" Dana screeched, eyes flashing. "She's *cuddly?* What kind of a person is that?"

The next event in the saga of Dana and Barry was a ski trip by the same faithful foursome, followed the very next weekend by a visit by Barry to Nashville. It surprised me, since they'd just been together, but, as usual, we planned a big family dinner.

After the meal, as we sat around the living room, I noticed that Dana was sitting on the floor by Barry's chair. Was I mistaken, or was she leaning against his leg? Was I mistaken, or was she looking at him like he was Tom Cruise? Was I mistaken, or every time he opened his mouth was she confusing him with Billy Graham?

Then the clincher! He reached out and stroked her hair! This in itself could be the eighth wonder of the world, because Dana cannot stand to have her hair touched. From the time she was a small child, her hair was off-limits. I always blamed it on the fact that she had such heavy hair that it actually gave her pain to have it messed with. Whatever the reason, you just didn't go there. But Barry was going there! And she was behaving like a dopey little kitten. She was loving it! She was all but purring!

Later, we pieced together the story. She had turned around on the ski slopes to see him skiing toward her, and her heart leaped out of her body. She threw him down right there in the snow, did heaven knows what (a mother *doesn't* want to know!), and the rest is history.

Like I always say, when it comes to your children, you should just bite your tongue and pray (knowing in your heart you have the answers). I just don't always take my own advice.

Diamonds and Dump Trucks

Judy Carden

Bob and I had just settled in for a short winter's nap when our three little cherubs exploded into our bedroom, bouncing up and down on our bed.

"Santa came! And he finished all of his cookies and milk," Aubrey squealed. "It's Christmas morning!" yelled Danny. "Hurry, hurry," five-year-old Ryan pleaded, bouncing high and landing smack in the middle of his father and me.

Fifteen minutes later, we were positioned around the Christmas tree, waiting to hear the magic words from Dad, *The first gift of Christmas goes to . . .* At long last, the festivities were under way.

Soft sounds of Christmas carols and squeals of delight filled the air, as, one by one, the children tore open their gifts.

Then came the moment when all eyes were on me, as Bob handed me a perfectly wrapped petite box.

"Open it," urged the children.

"Oooohh," I gasped, as I lifted a brilliant pair of diamond earrings from the box and put them in my ears. As I glanced around the room, though, I couldn't help but notice that the boys had exchanged worried glances. Danny smacked himself in the forehead and said, "Diamonds. Oh, no."

We continued our celebration until just one gift remained underneath the tree. It was clumsily wrapped, with much too much Scotch tape, and it had a tag that read "To Mom—from your boys."

For the second time that morning all eyes were on me as I ripped away at the layers of paper and tape and ceremoniously lifted their gift for all to see: a set of colorful plastic trucks! Three, to be exact.

"They're for me and you and Danny," Ryan informed me. "But they're not diamonds. Wanna play anyway?"

"They're better than diamonds," I said in between sobs.

And then I removed my earrings, grabbed a yellow dump truck, and said, "Last one to the sandbox is a rotten egg." Because, you know, diamonds are forever—but little boys are not.

What Did *You* Do Today?

Phil Callaway

I have been a husband for nearly ten years now, so needless to say I know virtually everything there is to know about my wife's needs. For instance, I know that she can get by without sleep for three days and three nights—but definitely not without chocolate. I also know that she needs flowers, nurturing, romance, protection, a listening ear, clean laundry, and clothes that fit. Whereas my basic needs are . . . well, pizza.

It is a quarter to five right now, and I'm sitting at my desk thinking about my need for pizza. It's been one of those days at the office. A computer blip swallowed half the morning's work, and nothing went right after that. I had no time for lunch. Deadlines loom. Reports beckon. And my stomach growls. It is saying, "Hey, give us pizza. We need pizza."

As the clock struggles toward 5:00 P.M., however, the growling is muffled in visions of home. Dinner will be store-bought Coke and homemade pizza. Toppings will include large hunks of pepperoni, layers of ham, and enough cheese to blanket Switzerland. The crust will be light, yet crunchy, flavored with a generous pinch of oregano. When I arrive, Ramona will be waiting at the door, her hair permed, her lips pursed. The children will be setting the table, newly washed smiles gracing each face. "Hi, Daddy!" they will say in unison. "We sure missed you."

Following dinner, the children will beg to be put to bed early. "We want you and Mom to have some time alone," they will say. "You've probably had a tough day."

As I park the car, however, I realize that something has gone terribly wrong. For one thing, half the neighborhood is in our yard. As I enter the house, I find the other half. They are riffling through our refrigerator. In the kitchen Ramona is bent over the dishwasher, cleaning out the last of the silverware. The table is piled high with laundry, and the stove holds not even a hint of supper.

Several times in my life I have said things people did not appreciate. This is one of those times.

"So what's for supper?" I ask. "Roast beef?"

There is silence.

I sit down beside the laundry and make an even bigger mistake. "So," I say, "what did *you* do today?"

Sometimes my wife moves very quickly. This is one of those times. Ramona stands up straight, brandishing a sharp fork.

"What did *I* do today?"

She walks swiftly across the room—still holding the fork.

"WHAT DID I DO TODAY?"

She hands me a piece of paper. A piece of paper women everywhere should own. Then she stands over me as I read it.

WHAT I DID TODAY

3:21 A.M.—Woke up. Took Jeffrey to bathroom.

3:31 A.M.—Woke up. Took Jeffrey back to bed.

3:46 A.M.—Got you to quit snoring.

3:49 A.M.—Went to sleep.

5:11 A.M.—Woke up. Took Jeffrey to bathroom.

6:50 A.M.—Alarm went off. Mentally reviewed all I had to do today.

7:00 A.M.—Alarm went off.

7:10 A.M.—Alarm went off. Contemplated doing something violent to alarm clock.

7:19 A.M.—Got up. Got dressed. Made bed. Warned Stephen.

7:20 A.M.—Warned Stephen.

7:21 A.M.—Spanked Stephen. Held Stephen. Prayed with Stephen.

7:29 A.M.–Fed boys a breakfast consisting of Cheerios, orange juice, and something that resembled toast. Scolded Jeffrey for mixing them.

7:35 A.M.–Woke Rachael.

7:38 A.M.–Had devotions.

7:49 A.M.–Made Stephen's lunch. Tried to answer Jeffrey's question, "Why does God need people?" Warned Stephen.

8:01 A.M.–Woke Rachael.

8:02 A.M.–Started laundry.

8:03 A.M.–Took rocks out of washing machine.

8:04 A.M.–Started laundry.

8:13 A.M.–Planned grocery list. Tried to answer Jeffrey's question "Why do we need God?"

8:29 A.M.–Woke Rachael (third time).

8:30 A.M.–Helped Stephen with homework.

8:31 A.M.–Sent Stephen to school. Told him to remember his lunch.

8:32 A.M.–Had breakfast with Rachael. Porridge.

Rest of morning–Took Stephen's lunch to him. Returned library books. Explained why a cover was missing. Mailed letters. Bought groceries. Shut TV off. Planned birthday party. Cleaned house. Wiped noses. Wiped windows. Wiped bottoms. Shut TV off. Cleaned spaghetti out of carpet. Cut bite marks off the cheese. Made owl-shaped sandwiches.

12:35 P.M.–Put wet clothes in dryer.

12:35 P.M.–Sat down to rest.

12:39 P.M.–Scolded Jeffrey. Helped him put clothes back in dryer.

12:45 P.M.–Agreed to baby-sit for a friend. Cut tree sap out of Rachael's hair. Regretted baby-sitting decision. Killed assorted insects. Read to the kids. Clipped ten fingernails. Sent kids outside. Unpacked groceries. Watered plants. Swept floor. Picked watermelon seeds off linoleum. Read to the kids.

3:43 P.M.—Stephen came home. Warned Stephen.

3:46 P.M.—Put Band-Aids on knees. Organized task force to clean kitchen. Cleaned parts of house. Accepted appointment to local committee (secretary said, "You probably have extra time since you don't work"). Tried to answer Rachael's question, "Why are boys and girls different?" Listened to a zillion more questions. Answered a few. Cleaned out dishwasher. Briefly considered running away from home.

5:21 P.M.—Husband arrived, looking for peace, perfection, and pizza.

I am finished reading now, but Ramona is not through. "Of course, not all my days go this smoothly," she says, still clutching the fork.

"Any questions?"

Often when Ramona and I are at public gatherings, she is asked The Question: "Do you work?" I'm glad she is not holding a fork at this point. Sometimes I wish she'd say, "Actually, I work days, nights, and weekends. How about you?" But she doesn't. She's a kind woman. She practices what I preach. Once, however, she confided that she wishes she had the eloquence to respond as one women did: "I am socializing three Homo sapiens in the dominant values of the Judeo-Christian tradition in order that they might be instruments for the transformation of the social order into the teleologically prescribed utopia inherent in the eschaton."

Then she would ask, "And what is it you do?"

Questions, Questions

Chris Ewing

It is my own fault, I suppose. Trying to instill a quest for learning in my children has led to my current sorry position of being in a growing state of educational inequality. In other words, I have reached the point where there are more questions I can't answer than there are ones that I can.

Remember the nursery rhyme "Twinkle, Twinkle, Little Star"? I changed it for my children in order to help foster the pursuit of science.

Twinkle, twinkle, little star,
How I wonder what you are.
Hydrogen gases swirling above,
Fusion fires that consume all love.
Twinkle, twinkle, little star,
Now we know just what you are.

My daughter asked, "Dad, if superconducting electromagnets generate magnetic fields millions of times stronger than the earth's, how come that doesn't mess up everyone's compasses?"

Hmm. Good question! Now, being a male and not wanting to display my ignorance in front of the children, I struggled for a plausible answer.

"Uh, well, by international law, I believe it is United Nations Mandate 4061, section 4, paragraph 13—and I quote: 'All large magnets, be they electrical in nature or not, must be installed so their magnetic poles align with those of the earth.' That keeps everything in sync, so there is no conflict in magnetic fields and all compasses remain pointing to their true polar direction." Whew! "Oh wow, Dad, you sure are smart."

The really tough questions, however, come from the youngest minds. "Daddy, what makes clouds?" *No problem,* I think.

"Well, when water evaporates, it rises into—"

"Daddy, what's 'vaporates mean?"

"E-vap-or-rates. That is when water turns into a vapor, which is kind of like a gas, and it goes into the air."

"Gas like you put in the car? From the gas 'tation?"

"Well, not really. The gas you put in the car is a liquid, like water." (I involuntarily wince at the memory of catching some youngster trying to fill the car's gas tank with the garden hose.) "But we will not EVER try to put water in the car again, will we?" I reinforced.

"Okay," he said. Sure. Right.

"Anyway, there are also gases that are like air. You just can't see them because the molecules are so far apart that they are invisible and you can see right through them."

"What are mol-kules?"

"Those are the little tiny pieces that make up everything in the world."

"Even me?"

"Even you."

"But will *I* become in-divisible?" This conversation had, as usual, rapidly gotten out of control.

"What?" I asked.

"Indivisible. So you can't see me anymore. Like the air."

"Oh. No, you don't get to be invisible until you are five years old." A shocked expression flashed across his face. "Kidding, just kidding," I quickly reassured. "You won't become invisible."

"But I want to be invisible!" he whined.

"Sorry! Sorry I tried to be nice and explain something to you! Now, do you want to know about clouds or not?"

"Yes," he sighed, "that is what I have been wanting and wanting!"

"All right. Clouds are just water that floats up in the air. When they get too much water in them, it rains or snows."

"Oh."

"And when clouds come down to the ground, that is fog." That perked him up.

"Then we get to drive in a cloud?"

"That's right."

"Cool!"

Sheesh. What it takes to get through to some people.

I recently attempted to assemble a toy my son had received for his birthday. In the instructions were words that made my blood run cold: "Some patience may be required." *Oh, great,* I thought. When something starts off like that, you instinctively know you are in trouble. And, as usual, the manufacturers understated the obvious. A *lot* of patience was required, and even then, the finished product didn't quite turn out as expected. Seems I had left out a tiny plastic piece—the one that had rolled off the table and was immediately gobbled up by the dog.

So it is with a family. "Some patience may be required" is an understatement. An unbelievable amount of commitment, hard work, and love is required—and things still never quite turn out as expected. We can just pray that the finished product is functional and durable and is something we can be proud of—even if a few little pieces have turned up missing.

Payback

Veda Boyd Jones

It didn't start out as revenge. Looking at the destruction around me, I said what mothers have said for centuries: "Wait until you have children of your own." My three sons swore they would never have offspring. In retaliation, I started a list of their misdeeds and told them that someday they will know what it was like to be on the receiving end. They protested that all their wrongdoings were accidents. But the list has been started.

As soon as the boys set up housekeeping, my husband, Jim, and I will knock calmly on the door. A 7.8 earthquake or a tornado will seem mild after Jim and I descend upon them with the list in hand.

We'll start screaming and arguing as soon as we enter the house, and it goes without saying that we'll be wearing gummy, black baseball cleats. Not only will we make marks on the kitchen floor, but we'll walk on the couch, too.

After we flip on every light in the house, we'll start at the top of the list. Clogging the toilet will be simple. There are several methods on the list to choose from. We can see if the Superman doll can overcome being flushed, or we can choose the more conventional manner and clog it with paper bathroom cups (so they won't know how many we've been using) or with a diaper or just three-fourths of a roll of toilet paper.

Armed with crayons, we'll draw pictures on the walls. I'm leaning toward a Picasso look-alike. Jim prefers pointillism. We'll use red Magic Marker in the middle of the tan carpet—where the couch can't be moved to hide it.

Spills are a cinch. I'll drop a jar of sweet pickles, one of honey, and another of apple juice on the kitchen floor. I'll leave the top off the popcorn popper so kernels and oil splatter everywhere. In the living room, Jim will knock over three full cups of hot chocolate with half-melted miniature marshmallows.

Jim and I have argued over the windows and have compromised, because we don't want to send the boys to bankruptcy court. We'll break only one window, but we'll make sure it's on the second floor.

We've also compromised about jumping on the beds. I don't mind the jumping, but I'm not going to hit my head on the window ledge and require stitches. We'll put ketchup instead of blood on the bedspread.

I'm not going to chop the bark off a redbud tree with a golf club, either. It doesn't seem right to hurt a living thing for the sake of a list and a promise, and I'm going to explain that to the boys. Our redbud is still living, but it's crippled and stands very lopsided. I couldn't do that to a tree.

But I will knock over a few plants. They always seem to survive a spilling, because they get new dirt in the clean-up process.

I hope the boys have screened-in porches. Jim gets the honor of knocking the screen door off the hinges (by accident, of course), since he always has to fix it. I'll just poke holes in the screens with Popsicle sticks so that insects—especially wasps—can get in.

Breaking a recliner will be a breeze. Jim and I will do that together so that one of us doesn't get hurt. We'll sit on the arms and talk, and we'll put our weight on the headrest until the chair turns over. I imagine it will take several falls, but we'll have plenty of time.

Speaking of time, we'll sneak into their bedrooms and set their alarms for 1:13 A.M. I never learned why they set our alarm for that special moment. That first night I thought I'd dreamed it. The second night I stayed up the next three hours wondering if it would go off again.

I wonder how the boys will feel about being pushed into the swimming pool—fully clothed, shoes on, and billfolds in back pockets?

There's something about boys. Parents who have a couple girls, even three, will have a different sort of life. For every girl, the mischief goes up linearly. With boys, the mischief is exponentially compounded.

My list will grow as the years go by, but I really hate to use it against the boys. I'd rather my sons just had children of their own.

And If I Die Before I Wake

Ken Davis

Parenting isn't for weaklings. Moms and dads must be stout of heart; they find that out quickly.

But there's one task that strikes fear and desperation into the toughest of them. You know the one: trying to enforce bedtime. Children have a deep, instinctive aversion to sleep. They'll climb any mountain, cross any river, swim any ocean, to avoid closing their eyes.

Our youngest daughter, Taryn, devised the strategy of calling out religious questions from the bedroom. It's the old Pharisee maneuver. One night, the fleeting tranquility of bedtime was broken by her inquiring mind's need to know. "Daddy, does God talk to us?" she shouted with Socratic intensity.

"Yes, God talks to us," I responded sagely. "Go to sleep. We'll discuss it in the morning." Being a fool. I imagined that would satisfy her.

"No, we must discuss it now!" Before I could frame an appropriate theological response, she added, "He said I could get up!"

How do you deal with that? Here's a child who doesn't know the meaning of the word *psychology,* and she's already deftly placed me in the palm of her hand, psyched out.

One night the bedtime battle reached epic proportions. It was a battle waged with weapons of quick wit and childish charm. In other words, I didn't stand a chance. I'd been struggling for thirty minutes, trying to get my other daughter, Traci, to settle down. Finally I put my foot down.

"Go to bed!" I commanded.

"I need a drink of water," Traci shot back without hesitation.

The verbal sparring match intensified. "You can't have water."

"Why?"

"You'll wet the bed."

"I've quit."

(How do they respond so quickly? Do they have a game plan? Do they pull random thoughts out of thin air? Is this the root of original sin? But I wasn't whipped yet.)

"You didn't quit wetting the bed," I countered. "You wet the bed just last night."

She was quick. "The cat did that!" She said it without hesitation, without blinking. Maybe she was going to be a lawyer.

I ignored the opportunity to laugh and embrace the teachable moment. Instead, I made my move to protect my authority. "Don't tell me the cat did it!" I bellowed. "The spot on your bed was the size of a large pizza! We only have a tiny little kitty."

"It wasn't our cat," she replied without missing a beat. She was a true professional; she was the best. Yes, she was going to be a lawyer.

And she was shocked—*shocked*—that I wouldn't believe her. I held her by the shoulders. "Look me in the eye," I insisted, "and tell me the truth."

Her bottom lip began to quiver, a huge martyr's tear welled up in her eye. "I'm sorry, Daddy," she sobbed. "But a big, giant cat took the screen off my window and jumped on my bed. He wet on my bed, and then he jumped back out the window." Sensing my skepticism, she continued. "He put the screen back on after he left; that's why it's still on now." I was speechless.

"He was a big cat!" she appended during my gaping silence.

I was coming to a slow boil. "I can't believe you'd lie to me like this." I scolded. "I want you to go straight to bed, and I don't want to hear a peep out of you." (I learned that one from my father. Evidently such sayings lose their power between generations; I could hear her in her bedroom making tiny little peeping sounds.)

Then, after a few moments of precious, lovely silence, a defiant little voice screeched from the bedroom. "Daddy, I want water, and I want it now!"

The gauntlet had been thrown down! My parental authority was up for grabs. I had only one option—I called on the sacred and hallowed words of parents across the reaches of time. "If I hear one more word from you," I roared, "I'll come in there and give you a spanking!"

"When you come," she sang out sweetly, "bring a glass of water."

I let out a great sigh, knowing when I was beaten. If *I* could think that quickly, I'd be a millionaire. "Go get your water," I laughed, "and then you get to bed or I'll come in there!"

But she wasn't done with me yet—not this night, not Traci. About twenty minutes later I realized I hadn't heard the pitter-patter of her little feet returning to bed. "Traci, what *are* you doing?" I called.

"Drinking water," she replied.

"No one can drink water for twenty minutes," I grumbled, as I stomped to the bathroom. I was wrong; children trying to avoid bedtime can do anything. These are the signs and wonders the Bible talks about in the Last Times. I opened the door and gazed upon a child who'd been quietly sipping water for twenty minutes. Her little belly looked like a basketball.

"You get to bed right this moment!" I barked.

This, of course, signaled a new phase in the negotiations. I closed my eyes and waited for the words I knew would come. They came. "I have to go to the bathroom."

Of course I had to let her go, or the giant cat would be back.

She still wasn't done with me. The next time I looked up, she was standing in the hallway, stark naked. She had her hands on her hips and that "whatcha gonna do about *this?*" look in her eye. Before I could respond, she took off. "Catch me!" she giggled as she zipped past me. I bolted out of my chair and bounded in clumsy pursuit, forgetting that God has equipped his naked children with the ability to turn on a dime.

She sprinted into the kitchen and hung a sharp right. I was wearing wool socks. On a linoleum floor with wool socks there is no such thing as a "sharp right." I lost control, spun out, and totaled my wife's new blender.

I walked away from the crash a bit shaken up, removing shards of glass from my body. Then, to my horror, I saw my naked daughter dash out the front door. What had started out as a power struggle between a parent and a child had now escalated into a neighborhood incident. This is how world wars begin. My daughter was running naked down the street, shattering the quiet of twilight as she sang, "Catch me! Catch me!"

I caught her about a block away from home. Then I remembered I was wearing only the moth-eaten woolen socks and a pair of old underwear.

I scooped up my giggling Godiva and ran the fastest hundred-yard dash of my life. Once back in the safety of our house, I laughed until it hurt.

I dared to inquire one day, "Whence cometh this dread of bed?"

"Monsters and prayers," said my daughter without looking up from her toys.

Monsters I understood. On more than one occasion I'd conspicuously sprayed "monster repellent" (water in an old Windex bottle) into the closet and under the bed to assure a safe night. But prayers? What could they possibly have to do with fear of the night?

The explanation forced me quickly out of the room. I needed to laugh without hurting her feelings. The child's prayer that begins "Now I lay me down to sleep" had been less than helpful during her formative years. One phrase in the prayer had embedded itself in her mind: "If I should die before I wake . . . " All the antics were to avoid that twilight zone where monsters live and people die.

CHAPTER EIGHT

Four-Legged Fun

They say a reasonable number of fleas is good fer a dog—
keeps him from broodin' over bein' a dog.
—Edward Noyes Westcott

One day two cats were watching a game of tennis.
"Hey," said the first cat, "I didn't know you liked tennis."

"Actually, I don't," responded the second cat. "The only reason
I'm remotely interested is because my father's in the racket."
—Anonymous

Dogs laugh, but they laugh with their tails.
What puts man in a higher state
of evolution is that he has got his laugh
on the right end.
—Max Eastman

What's That Smell?

Chonda Pierce

I wanted to kill that dog the first week we had him (which must be the terrible twos in dog years), but I didn't—but only for the children's sake.

My daughter, Chera, was eight years old when Disney did a remake of the movie *101 Dalmatians*. That Christmas she wanted a Dalmatian more than anything else in the world. Neither David nor I was too thrilled about something that eats and you-know-whats, but we figured a puppy would be easier to find than a Cabbage Patch doll.

Of course, I should have known when we picked out the puppy that he was going to be trouble, because the owner kept telling us how this was the last one of ten brothers and sisters. Why had everyone else skipped over him?

Since this was a Christmas present from Santa, David and I brought the pup home under cover of darkness.

"Maybe you can sing to him or something," said the woman who sold him to us. "To calm him down—since he's never ridden in a car."

I held the little freckled thing in my lap, wrapped in a blanket, and could feel him trembling through the covers. So as David drove, I began to sing, "You are my sunshine, my only sunshine." (It had worked for my son, Zachary, when *he* was two.)

The road back to our house was curvy, and one minute we were all leaning to the right, then we would straighten up, and then we would lean to the left. I was just singing about "how I had held you in my arms" when the little fellow bolted from my arms and landed on the dark floorboard where I couldn't see a thing but could feel him squirming around.

"Oops, he got away," I said.

"What do you mean *he got away?*" David asked. "He's in the car, isn't he?"

"Yes, but I mean I don't have him." I was groping in the blackness. "Turn on the light. He's somewhere down—"

"What's that smell?" asked David.

Then there came the loudest retching noise I'd ever heard from man or beast (and I have an older brother).

"Yuck! What's that smell?" David pulled onto the shoulder of the road and turned on the inside lights.

We found the tiny puppy standing there at my feet, trembling, surrounded by . . . well, let's just say everything was green and brown. David used an old piece of cardboard to clean up, although a shovel would have been better.

Not only did the new puppy get carsick, but he also was a whiner. We closed him off in the laundry room with a nice soft bed and plenty of water and food. But every time we walked away, he would whine.

"Shush," David begged, "Santa's coming tonight. Don't you want to be a good boy? Maybe Santa will bring you something." Not even the promise of goodies from the North Pole would shut up the dog. But when David went into the room to be with him, the puppy would lick his hand and stop whining.

"Oh," I said, "looks like he just wants to be with you."

"I could bring him to bed," David suggested.

"Or you could stay here with him," I voted.

So David slept on the floor of the laundry room on Christmas Eve—probably with visions of sugarplums dancing in his head. I tiptoed off to bed, and I heard him exclaim as I walked out of sight, "What's that awful smell?"

On Christmas morning David got up all red-eyed, his hair sticking out crazylike, but he had the video camera on his shoulder and was ready to go. When the children came racing down the steps, the little Dalmatian raced in a blur up the steps and right past them.

"What was that?" Chera wanted to know.

"It was a puppy!" Zach, who was four, cried out. "It was a puppy!"

They got to the bottom of the stairs and called the puppy. David kept the video rolling.

"What's he doing up there?" David asked.

Zach stood where he could peek up the stairs and answered, "Pee-peeing."

David grumbled.

"Come here!" Chera sang. "Come here, uh, boy? Girl?"

"Boy," David answered through his teeth.

"Come here, boy," Chera called out in her high-pitched voice, clapping her hands. The puppy raced out and tumbled down the steps and landed right on Chera's chest, knocking her back. He began to lick her face.

Zach petted him and said, "What's that smell?"

Right away Chera began to talk puppy talk, and the puppy seemed to understand. "Oh, you a good boyee. Yes, you are. Look at the little puppy. Oooooo! You such a happy puppy. Yes, you are. You like to lick my nose, don't you?"

"Ooo. He licked her nose!" cried Zach.

For the rest of the morning the puppy bounced around the house, up the stairs, down the stairs, under the tree, and over and through the mounds of wrapping paper. David followed him around with a wet cloth and some spray cleaner.

That night we watched *101 Dalmatians* (another of Chera's Christmas presents), and those puppies in the movie seemed so cute. They sat when they were supposed to, they ran where they were supposed to, and no one ever talked about how funny they smelled.

"So what are you going to name him?" I asked Chera after the movie was over. "How about Freckles? Or Pepper—like in the movie?" But Chera didn't seem to like either of those.

"Well, we have to call him something besides 'Hey-Boy,'" I pointed out.

"Naming a dog takes time," said David, holding a wet cloth. "The name has to fit, has to be just right—just right for Chera and . . . Hey-Boy. Me? I'd call him Leaky. But that's me. She'll come up with something that fits."

The dog almost didn't live long enough to be named. In the movie, the Dalmatians chewed up only the bad people's stuff, and everyone would clap and laugh at how clever they were. Our dog (Chewy would have been a good name) ate everything. When we went out, we left him closed up in the laundry room with plenty of food and water and a cozy bed, but that wasn't good enough for him. He chewed through the louvered door and went after the couch (Couch-Eater would have been another good name). He chewed off the sofa's front legs so that, when we arrived home, the couch had tilted forward and was lying facedown on the floor—dead. Couch-Eater had a cushion between his paws. That would have gone next, I'm sure, had we not interrupted.

During the next couple of weeks, the dog tore up a chunk of carpet (Carpet-Chomper, maybe), scratched the linoleum in the bathroom (Linoleum-Gouger), and ate the baseboard in the upstairs hallway (Baseboard-Muncher). I still don't know how he did that last one.

Then the day came when we were ready to move—to a house with a yard where we could drive a stake deep into the ground and tie a chain to it. "Bet he can't eat through that!" David said as he marched off to the hardware store to get what he needed to prepare our present home for sale. He came home with wood patch, carpet patch, a louver replacement kit, and a big throw rug to cover the hole in the living room. We stacked bricks under the front of the sofa—and then decided to abandon it. "Or we could take it along and let Hey-Boy use it as a chew toy," David suggested.

"I've got it!" Chera told us one day.

"Got what?" I asked.

"Got a name for him," she said, pointing to the spotted dog stretched out on his sofa, which barely was balanced on a couple of bricks.

"How about Smelly?" asked Zach, holding his nose.

"How about SPOT?" Chera said.

"Spot?" David asked.

"I get it!" said Zach. "Because he has spots!"

"No," said Chera. "Not Spot. S-P-O-T. SPOT. You told me, Dad, that his father's name was Sir Pepper. So we'll call him Sir Pepper Otis Theodore–SPOT!" She walked over and scratched the dog's belly, and he rolled over so she wouldn't miss a single spot. "Hey, SPOT," she said, "do you like that name?"

From then on his name was SPOT.

SPOT liked his new yard. David bought a doghouse and let the kids paint SPOT above the door. He put up a fence, and SPOT ran in circles in the yard until he beat a path around the edges. Sometimes David would plant bushes, and SPOT would dig them up. David would chase him around and around on the path the dog already had made. Sometimes SPOT would dig a hole under the fence and run off, and a neighbor would call to tell us that SPOT had just pottied on her bushes. Sometimes David called him names besides SPOT. I was sure that only confused the poor dog.

David and I could think of a dozen reasons we wanted to kill that dog. But then we had a couple of great reasons not to–Chera and Zachary. They loved that dog more than Nintendo and more than CDs. It didn't matter to them if SPOT chewed purses, dug holes, or tracked up the living room carpet. He could bark all night at a squirrel in a tree so that no one got any sleep, but they still loved that dog. We could go away for a week and come back in the middle of the night, and SPOT would jump up on the kids, lick their faces, and wag his tail. Zach would scratch him behind his ears, and Chera would talk her dog talk and SPOT would talk back to her.

One day I realized that what was playing out before me was unconditional love: I love you, no strings attached, no matter what. Since then, whenever I need to be reminded about unconditional love, I just watch those three together.

I've learned in my own life that it doesn't matter what I may have messed up–even if I tracked through the living room with big muddy footprints–God still loves me.

Unconditional Love–that would have been a good name for that crazy dog, too. But I don't think the doghouse was big enough to paint the name on it.

Help, Lord, There's a Cat on My Face!

Sheila Walsh

He will not let your foot slip—
he who watches over you will not slumber;
indeed, he who watches over Israel
will neither slumber nor sleep.

Psalm 121:3–4

With all my years of traveling, I've slept in some strange places. My great comfort when I'm far away from home is that the Lord never sleeps but always watches over me—whether I'm in Bangkok, Britain, or Boise, Idaho.

Some of the most powerful memories are from my days as a youth evangelist in Europe. In Britain, an evangelist or singer would never stay in a hotel after an evening meeting. Hospitality—and I use that word advisedly—would be extended from a member of the local church. That hospitality is what drove me to lift my eyes to my sleepless God to extend his help.

I remember staying with an old lady in Bristol, England, who had forty-three cats. I like cats, but forty-three are about forty-two cats too many for me. I drank my cup of cocoa with cat fur in it and then thanked my hostess and headed to bed.

"My little darlings will follow you!" she sang out after me.

I turned to see a plague of fur flow after me. "That's all right," I said. "I can find my room."

"It's where my darlings sleep, too!" She smiled as she delivered this good news.

Fluffy, Muffy, and the gang made themselves comfortable on the bed, in my suitcase, and in my toilet bag. We were a family.

As I went to sleep I prayed, "Lord, please keep these beasts off me while I'm sleeping."

I woke up to find that I was suffocating. I must be in a cave or a tunnel, I was drowning—no, it was worse than that. "Help, Lord, there's a cat on my face!"

Another town, another trauma. The couple that took me home after church seemed very nice—and almost normal. As we pulled into the driveway of their home, I listened, but not a bark or purr could be heard. Peace!

After supper the lady asked me if I minded sleeping in the garage. I said that was fine, assuming they had converted it into some sort of bedroom. But the man of the house pulled his car out of the garage and unfolded a camp bed in its place. It was November in England and very cold. I put on more clothes to go to bed than I had on during the day. (Where are forty-three cats when you need them?) Every thirty minutes the freezer would start up and *chug chug* till I longed for a cat to put in each ear.

In the morning, as I lay there stiff from cold and discomfort, the husband started his car to go to work and all the exhaust came flooding in. I thought, *I bet they're closet atheists, and they're trying to kill me!*

I stayed with a family in Holland for a week. They spoke no English, and I spoke no Dutch. The family shouted at me the whole time, apparently thinking it would make it easier for me to understand them.

I have lots of fun stories to tell and to laugh about in the comfort of my own home. But every story is held together by the common thread of God's faithfulness through it all. He was my constant companion.

Psalm 121 makes it clear that God never closes his eyes. He is always watching over you—and me—even if we sometimes get a little fur in our faces.

Hey, Dude!

John Ortberg

Sometime ago we went on vacation to a dude ranch in Arizona. My wife, Nancy, who grew up vacationing there, insisted that my experience would not be complete until I knew the exhilaration of a truly challenging horse ride. We went on a trail ride, but it was far too tame to count, as there was no possibility of falling and receiving a serious injury. The truth is that I have spent very little time around horses and have never actually met one I trusted, but of course I wasn't about to admit that.

So the next morning I rode out with five ranch hands to take the herd of horses to pasture about three miles away. I was very interested to meet my horse du jour. Often horses receive their name from some notable aspect of their temperament; when you get a horse named Pokey or Valium, you pretty much know what to expect. My horse was named Reverse, based on his particular eccentricity of going backward anytime someone was foolish enough to pull on his reins. I made a mental note not to do that.

The trip out to the pasture was uneventful. We dropped off the herd and were on our way back when one of the ranch hands decided to make a race of the return trip. His horse took off at full gallop, and the other four immediately started racing to catch up with him. Reverse started to make his move. Instinctively, I pulled on the reins as hard as I could. Reverse rose up on his hind legs and took a few steps backward—just as Silver used to do under the Lone Ranger—and then took off like a bat out of . . . a cannon.

For the better part of a mile, Reverse ran a dead heat. (The word *dead* sticks in my mind.) We were not sauntering or trotting—this was all-out sprinting as in a scene from a movie. The five ranch hands were college-age guys who lived on horseback all summer long, racing their horses as fast as they could. Reverse and I passed four of them. I say "Reverse and I," but the truth is, he was doing most of the work. I was just waiting to die. I was looking in the adjacent creek bed for the rock my head would split against once I was thrown off. Exodus 15:1 came to mind: "I will sing to the LORD, for he is highly exalted. The horse and its rider he has hurled into the sea."

While I was wondering how Nancy would spend the life insurance policy, the strangest thing happened. I realized there was a good chance I would survive this, and then it became one of the most exhilarating moments I had all week. I had a few moments of what Mihaly Csikszentmihalyi calls "flow"—my own private optimal experience. For a few moments I was completely captivated by a single activity. All I could hear was the pounding of Reverse's hooves; all I could feel was the rush of the wind in my face and the swaying rhythm of the gallop. Out of the corner of my eye, I could see the startled looks of the four horsemen of the apocalypse whom we passed up (a moment I enjoyed immensely). I felt *alive*—from my now-hatless head to the toes of my stirrup-straining feet. I started laughing from sheer adrenaline. By the time we pulled up to the fence, I knew this had been the ride of my life. I would not have missed this experience for anything.

Of course, when we pulled to a stop at the ranch (which, to my great relief, Reverse decided to do gradually), male pride would not allow me to indicate that this dash had been at all unplanned. "Yes, a decent mount," I said. "His wind isn't quite what it could be, perhaps, but never mind."

Anything for a Laugh

Marilyn Meberg

I wonder sometimes if God dreamed up certain creatures just for a laugh. For instance, there is a fish that sucks in air and then hiccups. Its hiccup can be heard by other fish a mile away. Wonder why God did that? I wonder if he laughs over it.

Then, of course, I wonder about the duck-billed platypus. When the first specimen was brought to England from Tasmania in 1880, the zoologists were mystified by the creature. Its two-foot-long body was covered with thick gray-brown hair (mammal?), but it had a flat tail (beaver?), webbed feet, and a wide rubbery bill (duck?)—and two spurs behind its rear ankles that secreted poison (snake?). The fact that this bizarre creature laid eggs caused the scientists to finally conclude that it must be a hoax. That theory was discarded, however, when a team of scientists discovered a whole pondful of platypuses in New South Wales. Those creatures could growl like dogs and lived most of their lives in the water, but they were also capable of climbing trees. Wonder what God was thinking? I wonder if platypuses make him laugh.

A little-known fact is that bedbugs bark when they smell human flesh. U.S. Army scientists came up with a scheme to use the bugs in Vietnam. The plan was to pack bedbugs in capsules rigged with miniature radio transmitters. The capsules were to be dropped on suspected Vietcong hideouts. If a radioman overheard their hungry barks, jets and artillery would be called in. The war ended, however, before the bugs saw active duty.

God is a wonder. I think he's also funny.

Cat Lovers Beware!

Patricia Wilson

I always dread the first ten seconds after my entrance into any gathering. That's how long it takes me to determine whether or not I know anyone in the room and whether or not we'll have anything to say to each other. At one end of the anxiety scale is not knowing a single soul in the room; at the other end is knowing only a single soul—and that soul not very well. Each situation calls for small talk. Long, in-depth discussions I can handle with aplomb, but I'd sooner hide in a corner all night than make small talk.

When I saw Phil waving at me from across the room, I heaved an inward sigh of relief. Although I didn't know Phil very well, I knew that he liked cats. His office was full of them, figuratively speaking. Posters of cats adorned the walls, stuffed cats sat on his chairs, and "catty" paraphernalia littered every available surface. Even his coffee mug was shaped like a cat! Being a cat lover of the first order myself, I knew we would have at least one subject in common.

No sooner had I joined him than Phil headed for the buffet and left me to chat with his wife, Tina. We talked generally about things like home renovating, living in the country, and raising kids and cats in the city.

"How many do you have?" Tina asked me.

"Well, I had three when Gerald and I were married and he had five, so we ended up with eight between us."

"Eight! How old were they?"

"My oldest fellow was ten, and Gerald's youngest was just two years old, and the rest fell in between."

She looked suitably impressed. "That must have been quite an adjustment."

"It was. At first, we had a lot of trouble with squabbling and spats, but eventually they got the pecking order sorted out, and they live together quite amiably now. Of course, there's still a flare-up now and then, but that's to be expected."

She smiled at me warmly. Encouraged, I continued on in my discourse. "It's not so bad now that we're down to four of them."

"Down to four!" She looked horrified. "What happened?"

"One of Gerald's boys was really homesick for his family in Montreal, so we agreed he could live with them. That left us seven at home."

She looked sympathetically at me. "You must have really missed him."

"Not really. I was just as glad to get the numbers down." A look of shock flashed across Tina's face. I ignored it and continued. "Anyway, within a short time, nature and attrition took care of the rest."

Tina's voice was warm with sympathy. She shook her head. "You're so brave about it. What happened to the others?"

I began to realize that she was a cat lover of the highest order. "Then we lost Vinnie—he was one of mine. Gerald found him in the barn, dead as a doornail. It looked as though he had fallen from one of the rafters. We were kind of surprised because they usually survive that kind of fall, but not poor Vinnie."

Her hand reached over and patted mine. Her brown eyes filled with tears. "It must have been a dreadful experience."

"Actually, I hadn't had Vinnie all that long, so it wasn't too bad. And we still had six left to keep us busy."

Tina's eyes narrowed, and she looked at me in puzzlement. I realized that I should be less flippant in my discussion on the demise of the cats. Trying to settle my face into a suitably somber expression, I continued on. "Then one of Gerald's older boys developed a terrible skin disease. We tried everything to cure it—it cost us a fortune in medical bills—but in the end, nothing could be done. We finally had to put him down."

"Put down!" Her voice mirrored the look of horror on her face.

I began to suspect that Phil's lady was rowing with one oar in the cat-lover's department. I answered her a little sharply. "Well, we didn't have much choice. There's only so much you can do, and then you have to be sensible about these things."

"Sensible!" She started to get up. "I think what you did is awful!"

"Well, so do I, but there comes a time when everyone has to make a decision like this. I had to do the same thing with an old dog of mine, and I cried for days afterward."

At this point, Phil returned from the buffet. "So, are you cat lovers comparing notes?" he asked cheerfully, obviously missing the look on Tina's face.

"We haven't gotten around to cats," Tina said tensely, "and I don't think I want to." She glared at me. "If this is how you treat your children, I'd hate to think about what you would do with your cats!"

CHAPTER NINE

A Little Bit Weird, a Whole Lot of Fun

The true object of all human life is play.
Earth is a task garden; heaven is a playground.
—G. K. Chesterton

That's the truest sign of insanity—
insane people are always sure they're just fine.
It's only the sane people
who are willing to admit
they're crazy.
—Nora Ephron

Air Bags, Seat Belts, and Change

Ken Davis

Ready for the day, I unbuckled my seat belt. I knelt on the front seat, bent over into the backseat, and began rummaging in the great junk-heap that constitutes the floor of my car.

I was desperately seeking my daily planner, which I often toss into the backseat rather than lugging it into the house. Without that book, sheer chaos was certain. I hadn't a clue where I was supposed to be or whom to call to find out where I was supposed to be. I didn't know what to do—my To-Do list was in the book. Everything was in the book. Without the book, my very existence could be called into question.

I was totally absorbed in rummaging through the artifacts on the floor. Half-eaten pizza, Happy Meal boxes, and sticky Dairy Queen cups flew in every direction. Did you know that if your face is on the carpet, your car could be accelerating down the street without your knowledge or permission? I didn't know that, either.

I'd accidentally left the vehicle in gear. My head was buried in the backseat, and my own backseat was elevated to headrest position. That sector of my anatomy, it should be noted, is sight-impaired.

I found the planner! Still facing backwards, I popped up with a victorious smirk. Then I noticed from the corner of my eye that various objects seemed to be moving slowly past the side window. Suddenly it hit me: My car was rolling! I spun quickly to stop the car, but a lamppost beat me to it.

Have you ever had your air bag go off?

I have, and I'm here to tell you it's nothing like TV commercials would have you believe. Those commercials present the air bag as something you'd activate purely for the entertainment value, like playing with a giant undulating marshmallow. Hollywood's special-effects wizards create this illusion by showing the deployment of the air bag in super–slow motion. Your kids beg you for a try. It looks like a great new ride for the amusement park.

My air bag wasn't even remotely like that. The slow motion must have been out of order. I didn't hear it coming, I didn't see it coming. It was just suddenly there. *Whap!* I had no idea what happened. All I knew was that my nose hurt worse than it had ever hurt in my life.

If I were designing cars, I'd install some kind of warning system. Perhaps one of those synthetic voices. "Your air bag is set to deploy in ten seconds," it would intone calmly. "We suggest you get out of the car."

After the air bag hit me, I kept my eyes closed for ten minutes. I had no choice in the matter—my glasses were embedded in my head. And I still had no clue what had happened. The car was full of powder, and the air bag had deflated. Through my tears, I only wondered why a huge hanky was now hanging from my steering wheel.

A bad word formed in the back of my head, stood up, and began making its way through the aisles and hallways of my brain, all the way to the front office where the lips are. Yes, it seemed almost certain I'd be starting my day with a curse. Now, I know what some of you are thinking: *No way! How could an inspirational author have a swearword in his head?*

Because I'm human, that's how. I still haven't reached that point in my pilgrimage where Scriptures come to my lips whenever my nose is broken. And my best guess is that you haven't, either. If I were to suddenly reach out of this book and punch you in the nose, I doubt that your reflex response would be, "Praise the Lord! I just want to thank God for your dynamic fist!"

If it's any comfort to you, the word in question never crossed the threshold of my lips. Before it came out, I started to laugh. I laughed until I cried. Why not? The tears were already there. For some reason, the term *air bag* took hold of me. What a ridiculous term! Twenty years ago no such phrase existed. Had I driven a car home and told my mother I had an air bag in my car, she would have responded in horror: "That's not a kind thing to say!"

How things change. What didn't exist yesterday is a household word today. As I laughed, my mind began to run free. (Don't worry; it has no air bags.) I began to laugh at my seat belt. When I was a child, there was no such term as *seat belt,* either. My mother was the safety device in our car. If I wanted to stand on the front seat, perch on the headrest, or drool out the window like our dog—no problem. In the event of an accident, my mother would save me with her arm.

Actually, it didn't even require an accident. Whenever she hit the brake, her arm would simultaneously arc toward me like a loose boom on a sailing ship. *Whap!* Talk about your tough love. "Why'd ya do that?" I'd snort through my bleeding nose.

"I kept you from going through the windshield," she'd reply with a look of heroic satisfaction.

"Can I go through the windshield next time?" I'd beg, still nursing my bleeding nose and sporting a shiner I'd never be able to explain to my friends. Very few kids, I believed, had ever died going through a windshield, but I suspected that thousands were victims of the long arm of the mom.

That's exactly why I loved riding with my grandma. She had that *thing* under her arm—that fleshy, soft forerunner to the air bag thing. When Grandma stepped on the brakes, her arm would come flying back, and I'd be smothered in gelatinous flesh. Everything would go black, and air would temporarily be cut off. But I didn't get hurt. Oh, I'd smell like Noxzema for a few days, but I could live with that.

My point is that nothing stays the same; everything changes. Grandma is no longer with us. If I understand heaven correctly, she no longer has the natural air bag. Automobiles have air bags, side-impact air bags, and switches for disengaging air bags. Parents are required to use infant seats to restrain children in cars. In my day, an infant seat was something you put a diaper on.

Change is everywhere. Even things that are dear to us change. Grandmas and grandpas die. Friends move away. The stock market falls. Only an unchanging God remains; he will never fail.

Coloring the Night Away

Marilyn Meberg

My friend Pat and I had agreed to spend the evening together, engaged in some wild and woolly activity yet to be determined. As we discussed various options, I became increasingly aware of my fatigue from a very demanding week. From that fatigue came a most soothing, novel, and appealing idea.

I announced to Pat, "I want to buy crayons and a coloring book and spend the evening coloring." She stared at me for a minute, trying to hide the look of incredulity on her face. Then, assuming her best therapist voice, she asked what kind of coloring book would please me and how many crayons I wanted. Pretending not to notice her clinical tone, I said I wanted at least twenty-four different colored crayons, and I would know the coloring book when I saw it.

With a kindly affirmation from Pat that spending the evening coloring might indeed be pleasant, she agreed to the plan. She did ask, however, if I thought smoking cigars while we colored would add a dimension of the adult to our activity. Since neither of us have the faintest notion of even how to smoke—much less how to smoke a cigar—we quickly gave up that idea as not only impractical but unappealing as well.

True to expectation I found the perfect coloring book for me. It was called *The Huckleberry Finn Coloring Book*. *Huckleberry Finn* has always been one of my favorite novels, and I was instantly gratified by my purchase. Pat chose a coloring book of Disney characters that I thought was a bit beneath her level of sophistication, but I didn't think it would be kind to say so.

Armed with my new coloring book and a box of twenty-four crayons (Pat had to buy her own; I told her I absolutely would *not* share mine), I settled down to one of the most soothing and delightful evenings I've had in ages. While I determined the perfect color combination for the Widow Douglas's dress, as well as for the apron of her sister, Miss Watson, we listened to Christmas music. Even though it wasn't yet Thanksgiving, and in spite of feeling slightly confused, I enjoyed it enormously.

I think it only fair to report that I was ready to quit coloring long before Pat was. In fact, I suspect she took up her crayons again after I left for home that evening.

I love the fact that God is a God who encourages *relationship*, not just with himself, but with one another. Jesus modeled that for us in the richness of his relationships with the twelve disciples. We are indeed rich when we have many friends, and I'm thoroughly convinced that God loves us, encourages us, nurtures us, and supports us through other human beings. They can almost become to us Jesus with skin.

May we not become so busy, harried, and overcommitted that we neglect that part of our soul that is fed and sustained by friendship.

Pacified

Patsy Clairmont

*When I was a child, I talked like a child, I thought
like a child, I reasoned like a child.*

1 Corinthians 13:11

Recently I had the most mirthful thought; it came to me during church. A man stood up during the service and walked down the aisle toward the back carrying his young child. The toddler obviously was not impressed with the sermon. To keep everyone from knowing the extent of the child's displeasure, the father had corked him. A pacifier protruded from the little one's mouth, keeping his fussiness firmly bottled. His face appeared a tad red from holding in his opinions, but the pacifier did seem to accomplish its purpose.

Now here's my thought: *I'd like to manufacture adult pacifiers.* What do you think? It makes me want to honk and to giggle. Too outrageous, you say? Well, not so quick.

Don't you know some pretty fussy people that you'd like to ... cork? C'mon now, be honest. Why, those rubber stoppers might prevent unnecessary dissension, promote goodwill among humankind, and even breed greater contentment. Are you catching the vision?

I can recall a number of times I should have taken a couple of good swigs on a pacifier instead of a couple of verbal swings at an antagonizer. We would all have been better off if I had. My joy certainly would have increased, for I have found that my first words are not always my finest choices. Instead, my reactive whirl of words has the capacity to be outlandish. More often than I'd like to admit, my verbal response is based in an unsteady emotion such as hurt. (And hurt can be as fickle as love.) In my attempt to hide my hurt and protect my vulnerable (and prideful) heart, I have used lashing language that puts others *en garde*. My reaction conveys an inaccurate message. It shouts "I'm angry" rather than confessing "I'm hurt."

Also, the sharp edge of lashing language can wound the recipient. In the heat of the moment, that can be somewhat satisfying. *Touché!* Yet, when our feelings cool off and our brains settle down, we almost always regret our knee-jerk (emphasis on *jerk*) reaction.

That's where the pacifiers fit in. Imagine how differently events would have unfolded if pacifiers had been applied appropriately. For example, picture Peter in the Garden of Gethsemane. Instead of whipping out his sword to whack off the soldier's ear, Peter would have raised his hand indicating a five-minute time-out. Then he'd reach for a small leather sack tied to his waist and pull out a well-worn pacifier. After several reflective pulls on his binkie, he would realize how inappropriate lashing out would be and instead turn to the Lord for direction.

See, this idea has merit. In fact, I can envision these teensy comforters being installed as standard equipment on automobiles. Honk, honk. Then, when the guy on the highway gets in our way, we push a button (instead of laying on the horn), which, in turn, releases our binkie from above our heads. We grab on to our pacifier, and after several deep slurps, we feel prepared to continue on our journey more ... well, pacified.

And what about school? Don't you think every high school should attach binkies to the desks? Then, when belligerence is the 'tude of the moment, teachers and students alike could unwind during a binkie break. Or maybe they could have a binkie room or a pacifier parlor instead of a detention hall. That way, the rebellious could ruminate rather than rumble.

I'd manufacture different colored pacifiers to go with our outfits, moods, and decor. I'd give the mouthpieces as gifts—tons of them. I'd offer them personalized, iridescent, flavored, and gold-trimmed. I'd organize pacifier conventions and even have marathons to reward the person who stays plugged the longest.

Only one thing niggles at me about this idea—the last words of 1 Corinthians 13:11: "I put childish ways behind me." Oh, phooey, that kinda spoils my frivolity.

How about you? Playing any childish games? Need to grow up?

Peculiarity Breeds Content

Becky Freeman

Do you really—I mean *really*—think so?" I asked my husband sincerely.

"Oh, Becky, *everybody* thinks so," Scott stated unequivocally.

So what was the subject of our discussion? It was my husband's opinion—and, according to him, the rest of the world's opinion—that I am a *peculiar* person.

It's not all that bad to be labeled "peculiar," really. Webster defines *peculiarity* as "something that belongs to only one person, thing, class, people; a distinguishing feature." I rather like that definition. *Unique* has a nicer ring to it, but *peculiar* will do just fine.

One of my most distinguishing features of late is my fingernails. You see—oh, how can I explain this?—I have none. There. I've admitted it. And I don't mean that they are short or bitten down to the nub. I mean, for the most part, they are nonexistent.

It all started when we went to the Christian Booksellers Convention in Denver, Colorado. Our publicist told my mother and me to be prepared to sign nearly two hundred copies of our book *Worms in My Tea*. "Wow!" I shouted into the phone. "Do you really think that many people will want to get copies of our book?"

"Oh, sure," she answered. "We're giving them away."

Well, even if it was a freebie-giveaway deal, the event still fell under the category of a "book signing." And if my hands would be on display for two hundred bookstore managers, I intended to make memorable encounters. I would begin by having my own nubby nails professionally covered up with the most beautiful fakes

I could afford. Thus innocently began a vicious cycle I am still coping with six months later.

From the day I walked into the beauty salon, I should have seen the handwriting on the wall. When the manicurist kept insisting that I relax, stating that I was one of the most tense manicures she'd ever sanded, I should have politely taken my leave. Instead, I courageously squeezed back tears and nodded toward the patch of blood oozing from my index finger directly beneath where Attila the Beautician's file was flying back and forth at warp speed. But I have to admit that, as soon as the swelling and bruises subsided (on my fingers, not the manicurist), my new set of acrylic nails indeed looked gorgeous.

By the time I arrived in Denver, I found myself using copious gestures when given the opportunity (yes, even making opportunities) for the sheer pleasure of waving my new nails around. Pointing was a great deal of fun. So was scratching Scott's neck. It wasn't until I was asked to sign an actual book that I realized there was going to be more to owning fingernails of length than I had bargained for. I came at the page, pen in hand, from a variety of angles. However, with my newly extended appendages, I may as well have been writing with a large pogo stick. My signature would not have passed preschool penmanship.

After signing the one hundredth book, I began to experience some success by squeezing the pen tightly between my knuckles. But my fingers eventually grew numb in that position, and I'm afraid it finally began to affect my thinking processes. Originally, my desire had been to come up with catchy individual greetings above my signature, like "Wormly Yours," "Love, Laughter, and Joy," and "May you find laughter in all your worms." I preferred that no two messages be exactly alike. After the one hundred fiftieth book, my mind began to wander, and I found myself writing odd salutations from bits of hymns I'd sung in childhood. I vaguely remember signing one book "All Glory, Laud, and Honor, Becky Freeman." I know the recipient of that copy is still shaking her head, wondering exactly what message I was trying to convey. I have no idea, but it was certainly heartfelt.

Scott took this new change in my hands' personality in stride—

until one night when he was trying to get to sleep and heard me crunching away on what he assumed was a bag of tortilla chips.

"Becky," he moaned, "cut it out. What are you eating at this time of night anyway?"

"My fake nails," I answered matter-of-factly. "Want a bite?"

I have never had a problem with nail-biting in my entire life. At least not until I acquired the artificial variety. Suddenly nail-biting took on an almost gourmet flavor. I've chewed off acrylic nails, gel nails, and plastic nails. All delicious. The problem is that, with each set of nails I bite off, my natural nails also peel off one layer at a time. My real nails now look as though my hands have been through a meat grinder, so I'm forced to cover them up when I go out in public. Now do you understand the vicious cycle I've begun?

You can see why my husband—and a few other people, too—have come to believe I am peculiar. I have to admit, since becoming a "real author," my life seems to be combing new depths of peculiarity. One moment I feel saucy and intelligent, ready to conquer the world—like Diane Sawyer. The next minute I am unpinning a dry-cleaning label from my dress while approaching the podium to speak—suddenly Minnie Pearl again.

I have been privileged to meet incredible people, and, at moments, I've even been treated as a near-celebrity. But 98 percent of the time I'm a housewife who lives in a cabin in the boonies with a husband, four kids, two dogs, a bathroom that needs scrubbing, and a frozen chicken that needs thawing.

Even though sophisticated people and agencies occasionally telephone our home/office/school/zoo now, I haven't even bothered to change the message on our answering machine to try to make us appear more businesslike. I mean, who do I think I could fool anyway? Executives and neighbors are all greeted by the identical message, delivered with as much Southern hospitality as I can dish out: "Hello, you've reached the home of the Freeman family and other wildlife." I side with Popeye the Sailorman on this point—"I am what I am."

And what does Scott think of all this? He shakes his head in wonder at what has transpired and pretends he has serious doubts about me and my grandiose adventures—at least in public. But my husband is always the first one I want to see after an exciting bit of news or an interesting encounter or an unusual experience or a new idea. Why? Because, in truth, no one—not one soul on the face of this earth—has shown as much pride and joy at the fact that I am a peculiar woman as has my own husband. He's consistently my best friend and cheerleader, even when my ideas seem harebrained to everyone else.

Just the other day, Scott and I took a walk together down our country road, holding hands. "Becky," he continued on a subject we discuss often, "you are *so* weird. I never met a person in my whole life as strange as you are. But you do intrigue me. When I come home, I don't know whether you're going to tell me you've got another book contract, or that you've run over the neighbor's mailbox, or that you tried to sterilize all our toothbrushes and ended up boiling them into one big plastic glob. I've got to stay around just to see what happens next."

Yes, we've finally accepted the fact that our love is a many-peculiared thing, but it took us a while to embrace it.

Traffic Ballet

Marilyn Meberg

This morning I was in my kitchen doing the mildly mindless things I do each day between 7:00 and 8:00 A.M. I flipped on *Good Morning America* to see if they knew anything I should and settled into my final cup of tea.

Am I ever glad I did! There was a segment that caused me to whoop with laughter and delight. I couldn't wait to tell you about it. In fact, I didn't even finish that cup of tea! I've dashed to my desk instead. Here's what set me off . . .

They interviewed a guy named Tony from Providence, Rhode Island, who is a traffic cop. He described how neither he nor any of the other guys on the traffic detail could bear one duty each of them had for at least an hour a day. They had to stand in the middle of a busy intersection directing traffic, and he said it was so boring and uneventful he could hardly endure it. He decided to try to spice up this dull task with something that would at least entertain himself and make the hour go faster.

He began experimenting with exaggerated hand and arm movements, which led to rhythmically syncopated body swings to go with the movements of his limbs. Finally, after only a few days, he began twirling from left to right, startling drivers with his flourishes of "hurry up," "slow down," or "stop!" It ultimately led to occasionally doing full body spins, which culminated in the splits.

Motorists grew to appreciate his antics so much that they honked and clapped until he had so many enthusiastic fans it created traffic jams, which only increased his need to twirl, flourish,

183

and point to get cars moving. To avoid the hazards his accumulation of fans presented, Tony was assigned to different intersections each day so no one would know for sure where he'd be performing.

As this interview was going on, we, the viewing audience, were treated to a video of Tony's "intersection ballet." Buses and cars were whizzing past in such proximity to him I wondered if he had ever been hit by any of the vehicles. The question was posed to Tony, and he said that he bounced off the side of a moving bus once because he lost his balance during one of his twirls. He said he suffered no bodily harm from the experience, but that it did inspire him to do a bit of practicing of his twirls in the basement of his home that night.

What a perfect example Tony is of how to practice a laugh lifestyle. A laugh lifestyle is predicated on our attitude toward the daily stuff of life. When those tasks seem too dull to endure, figure out a way to make them fun; get creative and entertain yourself. If the stuff of life for you right now is not dull and boring but instead painful and overwhelming, find something in the midst of the pain that makes you smile or helps you giggle anyway. There's always something somewhere—even if you just have to *pretend* to laugh until you really do!

You need that joy break, so take at least one every day. Hey, how about twirling and flourishing in your kitchen, grocery store, or office? It works for Tony.

Drunk without Drinking

Barbara Johnson

When I was preparing to undergo some minor surgery recently, the doctor warned me that the anesthesia might make me a little goofy, even hours after the surgery was completed. For a moment I wondered whether anyone who knew me and thought I was already pretty goofy would even notice. Then I remembered that it's my husband, Bill, who's the peculiar one, being an only child and all.

The doctor said that, when I left the hospital, I was not to drive a car, sign any contracts, or make any irrevocable decisions—because I would be considered legally drunk for twenty-four hours after the surgery. Never having had a drink of alcohol in my life, I had no idea what to expect. *Just think,* I told myself, *you're gonna be drunk without even taking a drink!*

The idea was so amazing to me that I started imagining I was drunk even before the surgery started. When I arrived at the out-patient desk, the receptionist shoved a stack of papers toward me and told me to "fill them out and check the things that apply, and then sign here, here, and here. Be sure to press hard because it's a triplicate form."

In my imaginary state of drunkenness, I had a little trouble following her rapid-fire instructions, but I finally completed them all. In just a moment the door opened, and a nurse called me in. As soon as she had me settled in a bed, three other nurses slipped through the curtain.

"Oh, Mrs. Johnson," one of them said in a low, excited voice, "we're so thrilled to have you here. When we saw your name on the admittance forms and realized it was you, we called you back early. All of us have read your books. I even have one of them here, and I was hoping you would sign it for me."

I wanted to beg off, pleading imaginary drunkenness, but she was a nurse—and she would know I hadn't had any anesthesia yet. So I signed her book and then looked expectantly at the four of them, wondering what would happen next.

They stood around my bed, their faces glowing with friendly smiles. Suddenly my little cubicle had taken on a party atmosphere. I wondered if it was because I was drunk—and then I remembered that I wasn't, at least not yet.

"Barb, could we pray with you before your surgery?" one of the nurses asked.

Enthusiastically, the four of them joined hands, and the two nearest to me clasped my hands in their own, and they prayed the sweetest prayer I'd ever heard. (Of course, I thought I was inebriated, so just about everything was sounding pretty good to me at that point!)

Outside the curtain, I heard a man clear his throat. "Oh, Dr. Brown!" one of the nurses said, peeking out of the curtain. "We're just saying a little prayer for Barb. Would you mind waiting a minute?"

Evidently he agreed, because she returned and the prayer continued.

In just a moment the nurses' prayers ended, and the anesthesiologist stepped up to my bed and gave me a reassuring pat on the arm. He, too, said a little prayer, asking God to be with all of us in that operating room. Under ordinary circumstances I might have become a little apprehensive, knowing that the moment had come for the surgery to commence. But he held my hand, and in my imaginary drunkenness—and having just heard the nurses pray for me so thoughtfully and sincerely—I managed to flash him a smile before the lights went out.

To be honest, I don't think I was ever "drunk" during those twenty-four hours after my surgery, but I certainly was on a high. I kept remembering those thoughtful nurses and how they had surrounded me with their love and held my hands in theirs—and then sent me off to lala land with their prayers echoing through my mind and filling my heart with peace. The joy that this memory brought me erased any discomfort the minor surgery might have caused.

By that evening, I was feeling fine—and even a little mischievous. Knowing that Bill had been warned by the doctor to beware of my expected intoxication, I could tell he was constantly watching me out of the corner of his eye. For just a moment, I was tempted to put a lampshade on my head and dance a jig on the sidewalk, and then call up a real-estate agent and sell the house. But just imagining how startled Bill would be was enough fun. And besides, being peculiar is *his* job.

If I Were in Charge of Voice Menus

Chonda Pierce

I had a great idea the other day. It came to me about ten minutes into a fifteen-minute wait on the telephone. I had just called the telephone company to add the call-waiting feature to my service. But when my ear began to ache (and my finger, too, from pushing all those buttons), I believed I had had enough call-waiting to last me for a long time and hung up.

That's when it hit me: Just think how much time I could save if I had some sort of calling menu on *my* phone. Why, I'd have time to do great things—sleep, for instance. Or I could take up fun and creative hobbies, like sleeping. (It's not that I'm lazy, but if I had enough sleep, then I could do really, really great things like clean my house.)

It took a long time to set up my menu selections, since I had a lot of prerecorded messages to record. (Of course, they weren't prerecorded until *after* I had recorded them. But wouldn't that make them *post*recorded?) Anyway, once I had the system set up, I was so excited to see how it would work that for the whole first day I just sat and listened to the calls come in.

Ring-Ring-Ring!

"Hello. This is Chonda. Welcome to my new voice menu system. I'm soooo excited about this and about the new freedoms and possibilities this brings to me as a working mother and wife and to you as someone who has lots of busy things to take care of and a desire to get on and off the phone as quickly as possible. To facilitate both our goals, please listen carefully to the following menu options and press firmly the button that most applies to the purpose of your call. I thank you from the bottom of my heart for being a big part of this new direction as I move into the new millennium. Just follow my directions. This will be easy, painless, and much faster than trying to call the water company just to ask how many days are in the current billing period."

I was trying to be light and humorous while at the same time taking a jab at what really gets my goat.

"If you would like to leave a simple message of 25 words or less for me, press one now. If you have an even shorter message for David or the children, press two now.

"If you are calling to make a delivery, press three now. If you are calling to make a delivery but you are lost, press four now.

"If you are my dentist calling to remind me of a cleaning I scheduled months ago and have simply forgotten all about, press 21 now, or if you've determined that a root canal is our only option, press 22 now.

"If you are calling to discuss the general happiness of my children, about their day in school, whether they've received all their shots and vaccinations, or about Zach's last report card, press 34 now.

"If you're calling because you don't think I'm raising my children correctly, you can hang up now.

"If you're calling because you'd like to go shopping, press 45 now.

"If you're calling because we went to high school together and you haven't seen me in years, but you happened to see me on TV this week and thought I could get you free tickets to the Grand Ole Opry this Saturday night, press 59 now.

"If you've dialed the wrong number, press 16 now.

"If you're calling to see if I'd be interested in buying either bottled water or a security system for my home, press 44 and then quickly step away from your telephone.

"If this is someone from my small group at church reminding me of our next meeting, press 38 now. Or press 39 if you know for sure we are having snacks.

"If this is Zachary's principal, sorry about that overhead projector. Press 84 now to listen to a more formal apology.

"If this is someone from the Gallup Poll, press 53 if you favor a voice menu like this, 54 if you disapprove, 55 if you strongly disapprove, and 56 if you did not get this far into the message.

"If you've never liked the Beatles, press 41.

"If you'd like to start a recycling program in your neighborhood, press 81.

"If you are currently involved in, or have a desire to learn more about, a carpooling program for any grade school children in the Barfield area, press 62.

"If we have ever been involved in the same carpooling program before, press 84 now to listen to a more formal apology.

"If you know of a good, quality facial soap that you would be willing to recommend, press 27.

"If you owe me any money at all, press 77 now. I'll get right back with you.

"If you love chain letters, press 51, then press any three numbers at random, and within a week you should receive at least a million phone calls from complete strangers.

"If you have any hot tips for *America's Most Wanted,* you'll have to press *66 and take an oath before continuing this call.

"If you have a hangnail that's been bugging you for some time, press 47. If it's a brand-new hangnail, press 46.

"If you have a family member who has a problem with rhinotillexomania, press 12. For a definition of rhinotillexomania, press 92. If you laugh, press 93.

"Mom, if that's you, press 67, then enter the number of times you have already called me this week and the percentage of those calls that have occurred before 7:00 A.M.

"If this is an emergency, press 69 and please hold for further instructions.

"If this message has made you late for any sort of meeting, press 84 to listen to a more formal apology.

"Thank you for your time and attention to these options. I wish only to make things convenient for you and myself—*especially* myself. As we continue to grow here, we will continue to update this menu, bringing you more and more options so that every need is met. If you would like to add other options, press 89 and leave some of your favorite numbers. If you'd like to talk with someone in person, that just won't be possible, so you'd better find a button to push. If you'd like to repeat this menu, press 99 now."

BEEP! Someone chose a button.

"Hello. This is Chonda. Welcome to my new voice menu system. I'm soo . . . "

I snatched up the telephone, "Mom, is that you?"

"Hi, honey," Mom answered.

"Why are you listening to this again?"

"I didn't catch it all the first time," she said. "What was that you said about Zachary's principal?"

After a little bit, I found out that my mother had a doctor's appointment scheduled for the next day (I made a note to enter that as button 33 later), and she was a bit worried about going by herself and talking with doctors who looked more at her chart, which was as fat as a phone book, than at her.

"I just like hearing your voice," she said. Taped or not, it didn't seem to matter to Mom. So I turned off the machine, and we talked for another hour. I guess I can put my housecleaning on hold.

Peanut Butter Yogurt and Raspberry Sauce

Marilyn Meberg

*Go and enjoy choice food and sweet drinks, and send
some to those who have nothing prepared.*
Nehemiah 8:10

One of the most delightfully peculiar experiences that will be forever squirreled away in my store of memories occurred some years ago when we were living in Fullerton, California.

I was indulging in one of my favorite taste treats—peanut butter frozen yogurt slathered with raspberry topping. As I was just dipping my spoon into this incomparable concoction, the door of the shop opened suddenly, and a tiny elderly lady burst through it. She scanned the shop for a second and then darted over to my table, pulled out the chair across from me, and sat down.

Before I had quite grasped what was happening, she leaned across the table and whispered, "Is anyone following me?" I looked suspiciously behind her and out into the parking lot from which she had emerged. Then I whispered back, "No, there's no one in sight."

"Good," she said, and with that she slipped out her teeth, snapped open her purse, and dropped the teeth into its depths.

Throughout this unexpected scene my spoon had remained frozen between my dish and my mouth. Galvanized into action by the melting of my yogurt, I put the spoon into my mouth. The little lady fixed her eyes on my spoon and then on my dish. I asked if she had ever eaten peanut butter yogurt with raspberry sauce. Without even looking at me, she said that she had wanted to try it all her life but never had. I calculated that "all her life" was probably some eighty years. I asked her if she'd like me to get her some.

Without a moment's hesitation, she said, "Yes," never taking her eyes off my yogurt. By the time I returned to our table with her order, she was nearly halfway through my original dish. I found this amusing, especially since she offered no explanation. I started eating what would have been hers, and we slurped along in companionable silence.

Across the street from where we were eating was an establishment for senior citizens that cared for those in fairly good health but in need of watching, as well as for those in poor health who needed constant attention. I classified my little yogurt companion as an inhabitant of this home. The minute she finished her yogurt, she began rapid preparations to leave. She whisked her teeth out from the environs of her purse, popped them in place, and headed for the door.

Concerned about her crossing the busy intersection alone, I asked if she'd let me accompany her. She was out the door and into the parking lot so fast I almost had to run to keep up with her. As I had surmised, she made her way into the senior citizens' building and scurried down the hall. The only thing she said to me was that she had to hurry or she'd miss lunch.

I stopped at the nurses' station and asked the girl behind the counter if she had noticed the little lady I had come with. She said, "Oh, yes. That's Felisha; she a real live wire." Then she asked if I happened to be a relative. I told her that Felisha and I had just met at the yogurt shop less than an hour ago. The girl's eyes twinkled as she asked, "Did you by any chance buy her a dish of yogurt?" I was a bit startled as I admitted that I had. The girl laughed and told me that Felisha knew every trick in the book.

I have revisited this memory many times throughout the years, not only for the deliciously quirky experience it provided, but for the example Felisha provided. Here's a little woman who knew how to get the most out of life—even to the point of my paying for it! I'll confess to you right now that Felisha is my model for "at the home" kind of living. When that day comes for me, I intend to join as many strangers as I can who will buy me peanut butter yogurt and raspberry sauce, or whatever else they may be eating. According to Nehemiah, that's a scriptural concept!

Live!

Luci Swindoll

I found a clever poem. I don't know who wrote it but there's a lot of the truth in it:

> *There was a very cautious man*
> *Who never laughed or played;*
> *He never risked, he never tried,*
> *He never sang or prayed.*
> *And when he one day passed away,*
> *His insurance was denied;*
> *For since he never really lived,*
> *They claim he never died.*

For those of us who "really live," it is hard to imagine why some people don't. I'm amazed at those who tell me they can't remember the last time they laughed. They confess, "We were never allowed to laugh in our home while I was growing up, so I just don't know how."

Playfulness is one of my favorite attributes in people. One morning a simple phone call cheered me up in the middle of paying bills. It was from some little kid who had the wrong number.

"Hello," I said.

"Hi."

"Well, hi, who is this?"

"Me."

"Oh—okay. Who would you like to speak with?"

"You."

"All right! How ya doin'?"

"Good. How *you* doin'?"

"I'm doing great. How old are you?"

"Four. How old are you?"

"I'm sixty. Would you like to marry me?"

"No. I gotta go now. You're too old. Bye."

"Bye."

You *may* feel too old to get married, but you should *never* feel too old to have fun. Laugh. Play. Risk. Try. Get out there, and really live!

Notes

The compilers acknowledge with gratitude the publishers and individuals who granted permission to reprint the stories found within the pages of this book. In a few cases, it was not possible to trace the original authors. The compilers will be happy to rectify this if and when the authors contact them by writing to Zondervan, 5300 Patterson Ave. S.E., Grand Rapids, MI 49530. Each piece is noted in the order it appears in the book.

"One Man's Treasure" is taken from *Wrestling for Remote Control*. Copyright © 1996 by G. Ron Darbee. Used by permission of Broadman & Holman Publishers.

"Light His Fire" is taken from *Marriage 911* by Becky Freeman. Copyright © 1996 by Becky Freeman. Used by permission.

"Pearly Gates" taken from *If You Want to Walk on Water, You've Got to Get Out of the Boat* by John Ortberg. Copyright © 2001 by John Ortberg. Used by permission of Zondervan.

"Pause for Concern" is taken from *Out on a Whim* by Dave Meurer. Copyright © 2001 by Dave Meurer. Used by permission, Bethany House Publishers.

"Showdown at the Hoedown" is taken from *Marriage 911* by Becky Freeman. Copyright © 1996 by Becky Freeman. Used by permission.

"A Day at the Beach" taken from *I Can See Myself in His Eyeballs* by Chonda Pierce. Copyright © 2001 by Chonda Pierce. Used by permission of Zondervan.

"Slapstick" is taken from *Marriage 911* by Becky Freeman. Copyright © 1996 by Becky Freeman. Used by permission.

"Kids: The Original Workout" taken from *Chonda Pierce on Her Soapbox* by Chonda Pierce. Copyright © 1999 by Chonda Pierce. Used by permission of Zondervan.

"Bet I Can!" taken from *The Best Devotions of Marilyn Meberg* by Marilyn Meberg. Copyright © 2001 by Marilyn Meberg. Used by permission of Zondervan.

"Yes, Ma'am!" by Sheila Walsh taken from *The Women of Faith Daily Devotional* by Patsy Clairmont, Barbara Johnson, Marilyn Meberg, Luci

"A River Runs Down It" is taken from *Mama Said There'd Be Days Like This* by Charlene Ann Baumbich. Copyright © 1995 by Charlene Ann Baumbich. Used by permission.

"Gourmet Goodies" is taken from *Sportin' a 'Tude* by Patsy Clairmont, a Focus on the Family book published by Tyndale House Publishers. Copyright © 1996 by Patsy Clairmont. All rights reserved. International copyright secured. Used by permission.

"Putting on the Ritz" is taken from *Silver in the Slop* by Cathy Lee Phillips, copyright © 1999 by Patchwork Press, P.O. Box 4684, Canton, GA 30115. Used by permission.

"The Trouble with Peanuts" by Barbara Johnson taken from *The Women of Faith Daily Devotional* by Patsy Clairmont, Barbara Johnson, Marilyn Meberg, Luci Swindoll, Sheila Walsh, and Thelma Wells. Copyright © 2002 by Women of Faith, Inc. Used by permission of Zondervan.

"Bare Witness" is taken from *I Used to Have Answers,* Now *I Have Kids*. Copyright © 2000 by Phil Callaway. Published by Harvest House Publishers, Eugene, OR 97402. Used by permission.

"Good Grief!" is taken from *Welcome to the Funny Farm* by Karen Scalf Linamen, Fleming H. Revell, a division of Baker Book House Company, copyright © 2001. Used by permission.

"Bite My Tongue!" taken from *Confessions of Four Friends Through Thick and Thin* by Gloria Gaither, Peggy Benson, Sue Buchanan, and Joy MacKenzie. Copyright © 2001 by Gloria Gaither, Peggy Benson, Sue Buchanan, and Joy MacKenzie. Used by permission of Zondervan.

"Diamonds and Dump Trucks," *God Things Come in Small Packages for Moms,* by Judy Carden, et al., 2000, Starburst Publishers, Lancaster, PA 17601 [www.starburstpublishers.com]. Used by permission.

"What Did *You* Do Today?" is taken from *I Used to Have Answers,* Now *I Have Kids*. Copyright © 2000 by Phil Callaway. Published by Harvest House Publishers, Eugene, OR 97402. Used by permission.

"Questions, Questions" by Chris Ewing is taken from *An Owner's Guide to Fatherhood,* published by Promise Press, an imprint of Barbour Publishing, Inc., Uhrichsville, Ohio. Used by permission.

"Payback" by Veda Boyd Jones. Copyright © 2002. Used by permission.

"And If I Die Before I Wake" taken from *Lighten Up!* by Ken Davis. Copyright © 2000 by Ken Davis. Used by permission of Zondervan.

"What's That Smell?" taken from *I Can See Myself in His Eyeballs* by Chonda Pierce. Copyright © 2001 by Chonda Pierce. Used by permission of Zondervan.

The Funniest Stories from Today's Funniest Women

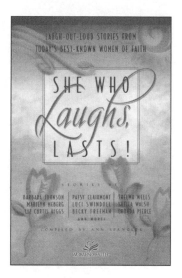

She Who Laughs, Lasts!

*Laugh-Out-Loud Stories from Today's
Best-Known Women of Faith*

Compiled by Ann Spangler

If you believe that "a cheerful heart is good medicine," then get ready for a potent prescription! *She Who Laughs, Lasts!* collects the funniest stories from today's funniest women of faith, who candidly recount their own foibles and follies as a way of reminding you that laughter can be faith's best friend.

Softcover 0-310-22898-0

Pick up a copy at your favorite bookstore today!

Soul-Stirring Stories to Lighten the Load and Strengthen the Heart

Don't Stop Laughing Now!
Stories to Tickle Your Funny Bone and Strengthen Your Faith
Compiled by Ann Spangler and Shari MacDonald

"The cheerful heart has a continual feast," says the author of Proverbs. *Don't Stop Laughing Now!* is the sequel to the best-selling *She Who Laughs, Lasts!* It offers the same winning recipe, blending laughter and inspiration into a delicious meal of fun and faith for readers hungry for more joy in their lives. Contributors include a variety of authors such as the hilarious Barbara Johnson, Patsy Clairmont, Chonda Pierce, and Becky Freeman. These true-to-life stories will take readers from giggles and laughter to heart-soothing tears and back again, infusing them with encouragement to help them make it through even the toughest day.

Softcover 0-310-23996-6

Pick up a copy at your favorite bookstore today!

ZONDERVAN™

GRAND RAPIDS, MICHIGAN 49530 USA

WWW.ZONDERVAN.COM

A Glimpse into the Lives of Old and New Testament Women

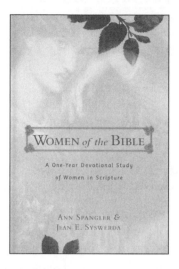

Women of the Bible
A One-Year Devotional Study of Women in Scripture
Ann Spangler and Jean E. Syswerda

Women of the Bible focuses on fifty-two remarkable women in Scripture—women whose struggles to live with faith and courage are not unlike our own. Far from being cardboard characters, these women encourage us through their failures as well as through their successes. You'll see how God acted in surprising and wonderful ways to draw them—and you—to himself.

This yearlong devotional offers a unique method to help you slow down and savor the story of God's unrelenting love for his people, offering a fresh perspective that will nourish and strengthen your personal communion with him.

Hardcover: 0-310-22352-0

Pick up a copy at your favorite bookstore today!

ZONDERVAN™

GRAND RAPIDS, MICHIGAN 49530 USA

WWW.ZONDERVAN.COM

Women of Today Can Find Inspiration and Encouragement in the Lives of the Women Who Lived in Bible Times

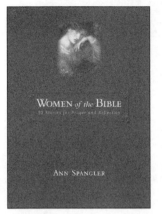

Women of the Bible:
52 Stories for Prayer and Reflection
Ann Spangler

These are the inspiring stories of 52 female characters in the Bible taken from the popular book *Women of the Bible*.

Women of the Bible: 52 Stories for Prayer and Reflection uses a weekly devotional format to offer contemporary Christian women an opportunity to study the legacies of women in Scripture. Some—such as Eve and Mary—are prominent and well-known biblical figures. But even the lives of the lesser-known women—such as Tamar, the daughter-in-law of Judah, who disguised herself as a prostitute—offer provocative and fascinating stories. What shines through in this inspirational book is the author's respect for these gritty, intelligent, and occasionally flawed women.

Each woman's life story is briefly recounted in an enchanting storytelling voice, helping readers see how these ancient stories still have meaning centuries later. Included is an introductory section listing each woman's name, her character, her sorrow, and her joy, as well as key Scriptures pertaining to her life. Then her story is told, followed by a section outlining her legacy of prayer.

Hardcover: 0-310-24493-5

Pick up a copy at your favorite bookstore today!

ZONDERVAN™

GRAND RAPIDS, MICHIGAN 49530 USA

WWW.ZONDERVAN.COM

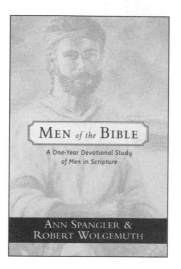

We want to hear from you. Please send your comments about this book to us in care of the address below. Thank you.

ZONDERVAN™

GRAND RAPIDS, MICHIGAN 49530 USA

WWW.ZONDERVAN.COM